HEARTLAND
New Mexico

HEARTLAND
NEW MEXICO

Photographs from the
Farm Security Administration,
1935–1943

Nancy Wood

University of New Mexico Press
Albuquerque

Also by Nancy Wood

Fiction
The King of Liberty Bend
The Last Five Dollar Baby
The Man Who Gave Thunder to the Earth

Poetry
Hollering Sun
Many Winters
War Cry on a Prayer Feather

Photography
In This Proud Land (with Roy Stryker)
The Grass Roots People
Taos Pueblo

Nonfiction
Clearcut: The Deforestation of America
Colorado: Big Mountain Country
When Buffalo Free the Mountains

Library of Congress Cataloging in Publication Data

Wood, Nancy C.
    Heartland New Mexico: photographs from the Farm
Security Administration, 1935–1943/Nancy Wood.
        p.   cm.
    Bibliography: p.
    ISBN 0-8263-1072-9
    1. New Mexico—Description and travel—Views.
2. New Mexico—Rural conditions—Pictorial works.
3. Cities and towns—New Mexico—Pictorial works.
I. United States. Farm Security Administration.
II. Title
F797.W66   1989
978.9'052—dc19
88-38519

*Frontispiece: Simon Potter
leads his pony across the
sage flats of Catron County,
1940. Russell Lee.*
LC-USF 33-12730-M5

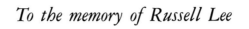

To the memory of Russell Lee

CONTENTS

ACKNOWLEDGMENTS

This book would not have been possible without the assistance and support of dozens of people. I would like to offer my deepest thanks to the following: at the Library of Congress: Leroy Bellamy, Beverly Brannon, and Steven Ostrow; at the University of New Mexico: Bill Tydeman, John Kessell, Gerald Nash, and Kevin Donovan. At the Museum of New Mexico, Steve Yates and David Turner were responsible for shuttling the FSA negatives back and forth between the Library of Congress and our printer in San Francisco. My editor, Dana Asbury, was endlessly helpful. Karen Embertson is to be commended for the book design.

The people of the three major areas covered by the FSA photographers contributed greatly to the text as well as to identification of many FSA subjects. In Mills and Bosque Farms, Milton Horn, my guide through the old Dust Bowl region, his sister Dale Jordan and her husband Jess, Albert Bada, and Ray and Myrtle Mitchell gave freely of their time and hospitality. In Pie Town, Rex and Patty Norris spent days showing me around the country and told me tales of the old days. Bob and Opal Magee, Roy and Maudie Belle McKee, Sam and Beverly Norris, George, Ollie, Pat, and Rose Hutton, and Edd Jones shared their stories and their hospitality. In Las Trampas, special thanks go to Bertha Lopez who introduced me to her many relatives, translated when necessary, and gave me a delicious basket of squash to take home. Father Walter Cassidy completed the background on Las Trampas for me by telling about his adventures there.

John Collier, Jr., detailed his FSA experiences, offered suggestions, and helped with picture selection. Mary Collier performed a labor of love when she spent three days typing the negative number list from the Library of Congress. Russell Lee gave of himself straight to the end. Master printer Edward Dyba of San Francisco did a superb job printing the FSA negatives of Collier, Lee, and Delano. The author is deeply grateful to the Taylor Museum of the Colorado Springs Fine Arts Center for their generous loan of six FSA photographs from their Southwestern collection.

Special thanks go to my researcher, Karen Schwehn, doctoral candidate in western history at the University of New Mexico. For their support and critical reading of the manuscript, I wish to thank my longtime friends, Carolyn Johnston and Robert W. Parker.

A literature grant from the National Endowment for the Arts enabled me to keep going during the time it took to write this book.

Preceding page: A farmer and his wife drive to town to do their weekly shopping. Taos County, 1939. Russell Lee.
LC-USF 34-34211-D

Opposite: Statues by a local artist. Cimarron, 1939. Arthur Rothstein.
LC-USF 33-12353-M2
LC-USF 34-34041-D

PREFACE

My involvement with this book began in 1962 when I first met Roy Stryker at the opening of the FSA exhibition, "The Bitter Years," at the Museum of Modern Art. Stryker, legendary director of the Farm Security Administration's historical section, stood amidst the giant prints selected for the show by Edward Steichen, a man he disliked intensely. The pictures that Steichen chose, without any consultation with Stryker, bothered him. They were mostly portraits of wiped-out sharecroppers and migrants, taken during the thirties when the nation was in the midst of a deep depression. "Goddammit," he fumed, his shock of white hair standing straight up, his large, expressive hands extending toward Dorothea Lange, Arthur Rothstein, Russell Lee, Walker Evans, and John Vachon, who were present, "that's not *all* they did." He wanted to

make his own statement about the positive side of the depression, and he asked me to help him.

We worked together off and on for ten years at his home in Grand Junction, Colorado, across the Rockies from where I lived in Colorado Springs. Eventually we produced *In This Proud Land,* which showed the upbeat side of America during the depression years. It was a place of laughter as well as tears, of triumph as well as defeat; the pictures that went into the book showed Stryker's firm belief in an enduring American culture. His was a biased view that did not attempt to balance geography, subject, or the work of a particular photographer. It was simply Stryker's choosing what he loved best from his personal collection, gathered before he left Washington in 1943.

Roy Stryker died in 1975. He never saw the photographic work that I began on my own when I received a grant to document the rural people of Colorado during its centennial year in 1976. How he would have loved it—an FSA project in miniature, complete with small towns, cultural artifacts, and hardy people who managed to hang on.

In 1984 Richard Rudisill and Arthur Olivas, two fine photo-archivists at the library of the Museum of New Mexico, urged me to do a book on the FSA in New Mexico. First I went to Washington and pored over more than 5,000 New Mexico images in the FSA file at the Library of Congress, eventually making more than 500 photocopies for consideration. I had not been through this file since 1972 when I examined the entire FSA print collection—some 70,000 in all—in order to help an ailing Stryker make his final selection for our book. On my return visit to the file I found that the New Mexico photographs are among the most evocative in the entire collection.

John Collier, Jr., and Russell Lee contributed greatly to the photographic selection process and gave me a background on their efforts in New Mexico for the FSA. For several summers Collier and I worked together in Taos, where he still comes to a modest adobe home he has had since the twenties when he was a struggling art stu-

Opposite: Russell Lee (left) and John Collier, Jr., sort through New Mexico Farm Security Administration photographs at the Museum of Fine Arts, Santa Fe, November 1985. Steven A. Yates, Museum of New Mexico.

Right: Roy Stryker. Angus McDougall.

dent there. Outspoken, critical, and inquisitive, Collier helped set the tone for the book.

Russell Lee met me in Lake City, Colorado, where he had spent forty summers trout fishing with his wife, Jean. Drinking our coffee in the mornings, sipping scotch in the afternoons, we sorted through pictures by the hour. On those he especially liked, he scrawled "MUST." In particular, the Pie Town series evoked memories of a happier time when he was at the height of his creative powers. The year before, Russell had learned he had bone cancer. Though in obvious pain, he worked hard until the job was done.

In November 1985, John Collier and Russell Lee got together in Santa Fe to make their final selections for the book. These two aging men had not seen each other for a long time, and their reunion was a joyful one. They sat and reminisced about their FSA days together, and exchanged Stryker stories and news about their wives. Jean Lee, a journalist, had accompanied Russell on most of his FSA trips, taking field notes and writing captions. Mary Collier, a Vassar graduate, once worked at the FSA office in Washington, helping to organize the file. Both women contributed much to their husbands' careers, though little recognition has come their way until now.

This book was a series of happy accidents as far as the field research was concerned. Despite misgivings that I would not find very much in Pie Town, I went to this remote village along the Continental Divide in May 1985. At the post office I found three men who remembered when Russell Lee arrived in the summer of 1940. Roy McKee, Rex Norris, and his bachelor brother Granville were all young homesteaders then. The four of us sat down at the local cafe with the FSA pictures, which triggered a flood of stories. Yes, they knew Faro Caudill (Lee's main subject) and said he'd gone to Alaska during the war, then became a big union boss in Albuquerque. They remembered Harmon Craig, who owned the town back in the twenties and gave everybody credit whether they had collateral or not. They recalled the meetings of the Literary Society and the all-day community sing. They remembered Jean and Russell Lee too, though they said they thought Russell was a German spy at the time.

I was certain that the Mills area, deep in the heart of New Mexico's former Dust Bowl, would be abandoned since it was already in decline when Dorothea Lange arrived in 1935. One cold February evening in 1987, I stopped at the Cat-tlemen's Cafe in Springer, about thirty-five miles from Mills. There I found three homesteader families—the Albert Badas, the Franklin Welches, and the Jess Jordans—having their usual Friday night supper together. They had all settled near Mills early in the century against unbelievable odds. They said that one old family was still left in the dying town. The next day Jess Jordan introduced me to Bobby Dennis, who remembered when Lange took her Dust Bowl series during the time when most families had already moved out.

At Bosque Farms, now a strip city twenty miles south of Albuquerque, I arrived feeling discouraged. The place bore no resemblance to the federally sponsored farm community photographed by Rothstein and Lange in the thirties. Now it had become an unattractive bedroom community, with fast-food restaurants, tract housing, and traffic rolling along a four-lane highway. A tip from one of the few remaining dairy farmers led me to eighty-five-year-old Ray Mitchell. He'd come from the Mills area, one of the dispossessed farmers that the government had introduced to the dairy business. He described the details of his life in the Dust Bowl and in Bosque Farms where he'd come to start over so many years ago.

In August 1986, John and Mary Collier and I went to Las Trampas and found ninety-year-old Juan Lopez whom John had photographed in 1943. Collier and Lopez experienced an emotional reunion, with both men speaking excitedly in Spanish. They had not seen each other in forty-three years. From this visit came the opportunity for me to become acquainted with other members of the Lopez-Romero families who trace their roots in the Las Trampas area back to the mid-eighteenth century when the town began.

Father Walter Cassidy, the parish priest from Peñasco photographed by Collier in 1943, was rumored to have died. My researcher, Karen Schwehn, discovered him in Albuquerque, caring for the people of the barrio. His older brother Philip, also a priest, was the one who had died years earlier. Father Cassidy regaled me with stories for an entire afternoon.

I came away from this project feeling that I had forged a link between then and now and, in the process, become changed by what I saw and felt. May this book be a lasting tribute to New Mexico's FSA photographers and their work.

Nancy Wood
Taos, New Mexico

Right: State line between Arizona and New Mexico, 1940. Arthur Rothstein.
LC-USF 34-24229-D

INTRODUCTION

The Farm Security Administration's photographic project of the thirties marked a turning point in the emerging documentary tradition that had its roots in the pictorial depiction of the Civil War. In 1935, when the FSA began, documentary photography was still a loose concept applied to work such as Mathew Brady's Civil War pictures, William Henry Jackson's photographs for the Hayden Survey, and to the efforts of Jacob Riis and Lewis Hine to show the evils of poverty and the exploitation of the poor. In Europe, nineteenth-century humanists like John Thomson, Eugene Atget, and August Sander had documented the essential character of their times in a direct, straightforward manner that was a startling contrast to the soft-focus romanticism popular in their day.

Paul Strand, who was one of Lewis Hine's students at the Ethical Culture School, presented a new and powerful approach to documentary photography as early as 1916 with his portraits of poor people on the streets of New York City. "Organic realism," as he called it, meant a point of view reflected in the faces, dress, and bearing of the people involved, the cultural artifacts—machines, signs, and houses—of their lives, and the natural landscape in which they lived.

By the mid-1930s, the documentary approach was thus already familiar ground. Newsreels, single-shot news photos, and crude 16-mm films reflected the disturbing conditions of the times. As a tool for social justice, however, documentary photography was still largely unexplored. Yet the ability of a photograph to influence people and events was already well established, ever since Jackson's work in the West helped create the national parks in the 1870s. The predicament of hungry, homeless, out-of-work people caught in the agony of the depression created the need for pictures to become a way of communicating both ideas and objectives.

In the summer of 1935 a rotund, bespectacled economics instructor from Columbia named Roy Stryker arrived in Washington to head up the Historical Section of the Resettlement Administration, forerunner of the FSA, for Rexford Tugwell, his old Columbia mentor who had become a member of Roosevelt's Brain Trust. Born in Kansas and reared on the Colorado frontier, Stryker developed a social consciousness at Columbia during the 1920s where he used the early work of Hine and Riis to hammer home his points for social justice. Though not a photographer himself, Stryker saw life with a photographer's eye for meaning, detail, and form. He soon began to see how the photographic concepts of Riis, Hine, and Strand could be applied to the problems of the depression, which in turn could be shown to an American public, then largely unaware of problems common throughout the land.

Roy Stryker started what would become the greatest documentary collection in the world with one photographer, Arthur Rothstein, his former student at Columbia. The young photographer was paid $1,620 a year and two cents a mile for his car, plus five dollars a day for room and board. Ignoring bureaucratic procedure, Stryker eventually hired ten more photographers according to his own high technical and aesthetic standards. "I don't give a hoot in hell for the bureaucracy," he once said, though he himself was immersed in one of the highest profile bureaucracies of the New Deal.

Stryker's small, often inexperienced, hand-picked group of photographers exceeded his wildest dreams. From 1935 to 1943, Dorothea Lange, Walker Evans, Arthur Rothstein, Russell Lee, Jack Delano, Carl Mydans, Theo Jung, John Vachon, John Collier, Jr., Marion Post Wolcott, and Ben Shahn roamed America recording the lives of farmers, migrants, and ordinary people caught in the Great Depression and, later, in the turmoil of the early years of World War II. They made a priceless photographic collection of a country and its people during a time of unprecedented change. As Stryker said later: "Out of America at peace grew the strength of America at war. This soil is the same soil and the people are the same people." Stryker and his photographers worked well together as a team, though the iconoclastic director has been given most of the credit for the project's success.

Stryker, who could be called the father of doc-

Opposite: Barbed wire fences make excellent clothes lines. Peñasco, 1943. John Collier, Jr.
LC-USW 3-17395-C

1

umentary photography, has also been called (by John Collier, Jr.) "a fanatic rural mystic." He understood the particular character of rural life, both seen and unseen, and how it shaped the culture of an entire region, such as the South. His own frontier roots, which included a stint as a cowboy, enabled him to empathize with the problems of rural Americans trying to hang on to the bare bones of existence. With an uncanny ability to determine relevance, Stryker insisted that his photographers capture what he called "the significant detail," meaning that special billboard, kitchen cupboard, or pair of work boots that revealed the essence of a person or a place. Toward that end he devised what he called a shooting script, assignment memos that were written as field guides for the photographers. A paternalistic Stryker also wrote detailed letters to his people in the field, telling them everything, from what kind of cameras to buy to where they ought to spend their vacations. John Collier, Jr., recalled that Stryker once told him to go to New England in the fall and "get the smell of burning leaves and hot apple pie cooling in the window."

Stryker also demanded that a photographer be thoroughly grounded in a subject before he sent

him into the field to cover it. Before he allowed Carl Mydans to photograph the cotton industry, he gave him a crash course in the subject. Recalled Stryker in 1972: "I told him about cotton as an agricultural product, cotton as a commercial product, the history of cotton in the South, and how it affected areas outside the country. By the time we were through, Carl was ready to go off and photograph cotton."

The FSA photographs became powerful tools for social reform during the Roosevelt era when passage of New Deal legislation depended upon graphic portrayal of the nation's needy. Rothstein's picture of a sun-bleached skull in the middle of badly eroded Dakota farmland, his photograph of a Dust Bowl farmer and his son fleeing a dust storm in Oklahoma, Lange's portrait of a poverty-stricken migrant mother, and Evans's searing images of Alabama sharecroppers became instant photographic icons in the 1930s through wide publication in magazines, newspapers, and books. They succeeded in arousing a nation's empathy and unlocking the congressional pocketbook to help rehabilitate citizens unable to help themselves. In the succeeding half-century, the FSA collection has come to symbolize the

Above: Evangelina Lopez grows and cans all her own vegetables for her family. Chamisal, 1940. Russell Lee. LC-USF 34-37140-D

Right: Corner of a living room in a Hispanic home. Taos County, 1939. Russell Lee. LC-USF 34-34410-D

tenacity and courage of a people trying to survive the worst of times. The FSA archive represents a milestone in photography, unsurpassed in its depth and scope, though several attempts have been made at imitating the Stryker/FSA technique.

Yet throughout the eight-year tenure of the FSA, which became the Office of War Information (OWI) in 1942, Roy Stryker struggled to keep his small unit alive. Budget cuts and bureaucratic infighting reduced his staff to two (Rothstein and Lee) in 1938, and more than once the whole project was threatened with oblivion. At times, over Stryker's vehement objections, the photographers were forced to make mundane illustrations of dam building, sorghum fields, and irrigation projects for the Department of Agriculture and other federal agencies. The choice, humanistic pictures that have come to symbolize the FSA Historical Section actually amount to less than 25 percent of the more than 270,000 negatives taken during the project's lifetime.

When Stryker was about to leave OWI in 1943 to become director of photography for Standard Oil of New Jersey, the FSA negatives and prints were boxed up, destined for shipment to the government dump in Virginia. Only direct intervention by President Roosevelt saved the collection at the last moment. Under the care of Stryker's old friend, poet Archibald MacLeish, then Librarian of Congress, the FSA file went to the Library of Congress where it was eventually given a permanent home.

Was it the era, the place, the people, or the photographers that made the FSA project unique? More than fifty years have passed since Arthur Rothstein shot the first pictures for the FSA file, and still the mystique of these photographs remains. They are now in galleries and museums worldwide; there have been dozens of books on the FSA, countless articles, several films, a plethora of dissertations, and the kind of scholarly seminars that Roy Stryker found pretentious. He wanted his pictures to be seen, not talked about; he believed that all he was doing was "creating an encyclopedia of American agriculture." Yet the FSA photographs go beyond encyclopedias, art, history, photography, or anthropology.

They connect Americans to one another. They make people laugh. They create a nostalgia for the kind of uncomplicated innocence that perhaps the country never really had. And yet, the photographs spell it out. Details of kitchens. Backyards. Store windows. One-room

schoolhouses. Parlors. Soda jerks. Migrants. Storekeepers. Gamblers. Schoolchildren. Fortune-tellers. Old ladies with sturdy shoes, black leather purses, long, baggy dresses, low-crowned hats with veils, and faces that reflect an indomitable will. The pictures show suffering and despair, but they show a singular courage, too.

THE FSA PHOTOGRAPHERS IN NEW MEXICO

New Mexico was never singled out by Roy Stryker as a state deserving in-depth fieldwork during the thirties, mainly because New Deal efforts centered around the South, the Midwest, and California. Stryker had no budget to send photographers to marginal, sparsely populated states like New Mexico until the later years of the project.

Dust Bowl coverage of the eastern plains of New Mexico by Dorothea Lange and Arthur Rothstein, in 1935 and 1936 respectively, was a geographic accident; each photographer was crisscrossing the hard-hit Texas and Oklahoma Panhandle where the Dust Bowl was the worst. Rothstein and Lange each made brief stops in the Mills area, but no record exists about why they were there. An assignment to photograph gov-

Opposite: A model T Ford, used by many Dust Bowl refugees, requires constant attention. Pie Town, 1940. Russell Lee.
LC-USF 34-36722-D

Above: Mrs. Bill Stagg draws water from her indoor well. Pie Town, 1940. Russell Lee.
LC-USF 34-36667-D

Below: The Whinery children make do with sawhorses and crates as they play house in their backyard. Pie Town, 1940. Russell Lee.
LC-USF 33-12744-M4

Overleaf: This farmstead was part of the Las Trampas land grant, awarded in 1751 by the king of Spain. Chamisal, 1940. Russell Lee.
LC-USF 34-37100-D

ernment-sponsored rehabilitation farms led Lange to Bosque Farms in December 1935, the same period during which she made her unforgettable series of stalled and destitute migrants along U.S. 70 between Roswell and Deming. Rothstein arrived in Bosque Farms in the spring of 1936 and took up where Lange left off in showing how rehabilitation clients were adjusting to their new lives. Other photographs made by Rothstein were of the Rio Grande Valley, Taos Pueblo, and the Mescalero Apache reservation, but these seem random and not part of any specific FSA assignment. Indeed, some of the most poignant pictures in the FSA file are not part of any assignment at all, but simply reflect the photographers' own deep concern for the human condition.

Despite the opportunity that existed in New Mexico, the plight of the Indian was not high on Stryker's list of priorities. When John Collier, Commissioner of Indian Affairs and the father of FSA photographer John Collier, Jr., was trying to force passage of his own Indian New Deal legislation in 1936, Stryker was busy sending his photographers to Appalachia, the Deep South, and California. As John Collier, Jr., noted in a 1985 interview: "Basically, Stryker was not interested in Indians and their problems." However, Collier was sent to Taos Pueblo in January 1943 to photograph what Stryker called "the oldest democracy in America" at a time when OWI was intent on developing picture stories to show the strengths of wartime America on the homefront.

Collier, who has achieved an international reputation for creating what he calls "visual anthropology," joined the FSA team in August 1941, the last photographer hired by Stryker. His first job was making mundane illustrations of soil erosion and plant growth "with a fountain pen for scale lying in the foreground." Soon he graduated to taking "ethnic" pictures of Portuguese fishermen, Amish farmers, and Hispanic villagers that are among the most powerful in the file. In 1986 he analyzed the duties—and attitudes—of the FSA photographers when he wrote:

> We fulfilled the informational needs, meticulously photographing soil washed from improperly cultivated fields, and improperly canned green beans. But in between these official duties we worked for Roy Stryker whose concerns were the "good life" and American rural culture. He consistently challenged his team to go beyond the accepted limits of photography to record the extra-sensory nuances of environment. Stryker was always pushing for a fresh and original regional view. He was an unusual scholar—part

geographer, part agricultural economist, part American historian. And beneath all this, Roy was a cowboy from Colorado!

During the entire FSA period, Stryker gathered an informal but dedicated photographic team, all with fine arts or music backgrounds, but all dedicated to the "human condition"—extremists who would go to far ends to make profound documentations. Stryker's photographers were also the delight of harassed county agents, for we were human enthusiasts and we gave harried field workers stimulation and appreciation. What we gathered in eight years was a unique visual geography of America covering every element of rural and small town life—participant observation, photographs made over a collaborative human bridge. How many family meals are there in the FSA file, from Acadian Maine to Hispanic Southwest, with an empty plate in the foreground, each waiting for the photographer to sit down?

Despite such hindsight appraisal of the lofty ideals of the FSA photographers and Roy Stryker's humanitarian goals, New Mexico's problems were ignored for the first four years of the agency's life. By 1939, when the worst of the depression was over, Stryker finally sent Russell Lee to photograph Hispanic villages, though his intent seemed to reflect a patronizing attitude that included stereotypes of the western image. Lee's first directive from Stryker said:

We are certainly looking forward to seeing the pictures which you are getting in the upper Rio Grande valley and in and around Taos. Don't forget a good ranch to go along with some of the more impoverished and small subsistence ranches. A few pictorial shots, please, such as: a row of Lombardy poplar trees with clouds in the background; shots of juniper and other trees, flowers in the background. Don't forget the picture of sagebrush you were going to get for me; a sheepherder and sheep on a hill, silhouetted against the sky; don't forget that the burro is an important part of that agriculture—we could stand quite a few shots of the little animal, taken in various poses and in various types of work in which he helps; a few pictures of the adobe churches. . . .

The following year, Lee returned to Chamisal, Peñasco, and Taos to finish documenting Hispanic village life. Excitedly, he wrote to Stryker that he had been successful in getting pictures of

life around a Spanish-American home—mostly the duties of a housewife—from feeding the rabbits, gathering vegetables in the garden, making soap at home, preparing tortillas, chile peppers and the like. Yesterday we went to

Above: An FSA client stirs a kettle of soap. Taos County, 1939. Russell Lee.
LC-USF 33-12405-M1

Right: A woman bakes bread in a horno, *introduced by the Spanish in the seventeenth century. Taos County, 1939. Russell Lee.*
LC-USF 34-34215-D

another place where the Grandmother (age 75) went through all the motions of baking bread in an outdoor oven. . . . Also got pix of their house—inside and out—it was one of the neatest I have been in. The people are really grand around here—but I sure wish I had a knowledge of Spanish.

Lee's thorough work in Peñasco and Chamisal in 1939 and 1940 was intended by Stryker to become a book on Hispanic life, but it was not published until 1985.* The war effort eclipsed Stryker's interest in producing such a book, and Lee went on to serve as an aerial photographer during the war.

Lee's famous series on Pie Town was made purely by accident. In June of 1940, Lee and his wife, Jean, had finished up extensive documentation of Texas and were on their way to photograph in Peñasco and Chamisal. Stopping at a cafe in Socorro, Lee became intrigued by the strange name, *Pie Town,* on the map. In a 1985 interview he said:

> So we decided to take a little detour [on the way to Peñasco]. We had just done Texas and we had this big shoot [of Hispanic villages] coming up. We thought we'd go over and relax,

Russell Lee's FSA Photographs of Chamisal and Peñasco, edited by William Wroth. Santa Fe: Ancient City Press.

you know, there it was on the Continental Divide. Pie Town turned out to be this wonderful frontier town, much like the frontier towns of a century ago. I got very excited about it because, it seemed to me, this was the sort of place that had unalterably molded the American character. Roy said, "Go ahead and do it and while you're there, you might as well check out mining." So that's how I covered Mogollon, too.

Lee's "detour" lasted three weeks.

Pie Town was an intense, creative time for the young couple. While Russell took pictures day after day, Jean wrote notes about the land, the people, and the town, and sent them back to Washington with Russell's negatives. No trace of them has ever been found. The Pie Town series touched a responsive chord in Americans gearing up for war. The simple, hard-working home-

Above left: Diego Lovato repairs his wife's shoe. *Chamisal, 1940. Russell Lee.* LC-USF 34-37018-D

Above right: Daughter of an FSA client hauls water from the family well. Taos County, 1939. Russell Lee. LC-USF 33-12426-M3

Right: Enjaradoras *replaster adobe houses every year, first using trowels to apply wet mud, then smoothing out the surface by hand. Chamisal, 1939. Russell Lee.* LC-USF 34-37082-D

Opposite: Gold miner at
the end of a day's work.
Mogollon, 1940. Russell
Lee.
LC-USF 33-12759-M4

Above: Barroom on payday
in Mogollon, 1940.
Russell Lee.
LC-USF 34-36836-D

Below: Main street of
Mogollon, the second
largest gold mining town
in the state, 1940. Russell
Lee. LC-USF 34-36528-D

steaders depicted by Lee represented a part of frontier America that would soon fade into history; so, too, did the Hispanic villages that Lee covered the following month. The Second World War not only brought about a loss of the traditions photographed by Lee, but also opened the way for modernization of these villages. Neither Pie Town nor the Hispanic villages would ever be the same. Shortly before he died, Russell Lee said: "I didn't know at the time how important those pictures [of Pie Town] would be. I didn't know there would be such a fuss over Peñasco and Chamisal. I thought I was making a record, that's all."

The record of Hispanic life begun by Lee in 1939 and 1940 was rounded out by John Collier, Jr., in January 1943. "I went to the county agent in Taos," recalled Collier in a 1987 interview.

> I asked him what was happening. Of course it was January. There was snow on the ground, so I couldn't photograph spring planting or build-

ing irrigation ditches, the sorts of things that Roy liked. I couldn't go back empty-handed, so I went to Questa and hooked up with the parish priest, Father Smith. I did the same thing in Peñasco with Father Cassidy.

Through these two parish priests, Collier was able to find the introduction he needed into the Hispanic culture of New Mexico. While Lee concentrated on the everyday activities of the villages (bread making, plastering, butchering), Collier focused more on family and religious life. The combination of the two photographers' work reveals in intimate detail the rich, complex Hispanic culture of New Mexico during the war and prewar years.

Before he returned to Washington, Collier also photographed several Anglo ranch families in the Moreno Valley, which rounded out his work in New Mexico. Collier, as well as Lee, went on to work with Stryker at Standard Oil of New Jersey after the war, helping to build a file nearly as diverse as that of the FSA.

Opposite: John Mutz, cattleman, heads out in a blizzard. Moreno Valley, 1943. John Collier, Jr. LC-USF 34-18900-E

Above: Repairing adobe haciendas is an ongoing job. Here, two men fix the tin roof of a house near Chacon, 1943. John Collier, Jr. LC-USF 34-14715-C

Below: José Fresquez spends his spare time reading on the sunny enclosed porch of his home. Chamisal, 1940. Russell Lee. LC-USF 34-37145-D

Two other FSA photographers made brief appearances in New Mexico. Jack Delano, by then famous for his shots of Greene County, Georgia, Portuguese fishermen on the coast, and rural life in New England, was assigned to cover the Santa Fe railroad in 1943. "The railroad was part of the American scene," said Delano in a 1985 interview. "It was essential to the war effort. And Stryker just happened to like trains." Delano was assigned to photograph the Santa Fe line from Texas to California, but he seldom got off the train to photograph the little towns through which he passed. His assignment was not to investigate these towns or their people, but to prepare a photographic essay on the importance of the railroad and its workers during the height of the war effort.

John Vachon, who had majored in Elizabethan poetry in college, was first a messenger boy for the FSA, then was added to the photographic staff in 1937. While on an extended assignment to cover the West in 1942, he happened to pass through the oil boomtown of Hobbs. His static shots of Hobbs do not reveal the same character of the town captured by Russell Lee in March 1940, just before making a swing through Texas.

Opposite: On the Atchison, Topeka and Santa Fe railroad line. Grants, 1943. Jack Delano.
LC-USW 3-22182-D

Above: Almeta Williams, employed by the Atchison, Topeka and Santa Fe railroad yard to clean out potash cars. Clovis, 1943. Jack Delano.
LC-USW 3-20607-E

Left: Cot houses are for
workers pouring into the
area to work in the oil
fields. Hobbs, 1940.
Russell Lee.
LC-USF 34-35816-D

Below: Main street.
Hobbs, 1940. Russell Lee.
LC-USF 34-35845-D

Right: Signs in an oil
boomtown. Hobbs, 1940.
Russell Lee.
LC-USF 34-35815-D

To Lee, Hobbs had one of the state's more colorful pasts. During Prohibition, numerous taverns
—roller skating rinks by day and dance halls at
night—were opened. Brothels, domino parlors,
nineteen pool halls, and other gambling spots
flourished, drawing many "undesirables" into
town. An all-metal tank, chained to posts and
set in the sun, served as the local jail, while
prisoners with "infectious diseases" were kept in
the "pesthouse."

By the time that Russell Lee photographed
Hobbs, its bawdiness had disappeared. It was, he
later recalled, "a nice little town with wide
streets, friendly people, a lot of dust and oil der-
ricks. It reminded me a lot of Texas." In the
twenties, however, when oil dropped to ten cents
a barrel, more than three-fourths of the population left, their temporary houses lifted onto truck
beds and hauled off. With improved technology
and increased demand for oil, Hobbs soon
revived and is today still a boomtown, albeit one
without the rough edges of its previous heyday.

The work of the FSA photographers in New Mexico turned out to be among the most important in the file, connecting diverse cultures, landscapes, and people. As Roy Stryker wrote in our book, *In This Proud Land:* "We succeeded in doing exactly what Rex Tugwell said we should do: *We introduced Americans to America. . . .* The full effect of this team's work was that it helped connect one generation's image of itself with the reality of its own time in history."

NEW MEXICO IN THE DEPRESSION YEARS

The ravaging effects of the depression were felt throughout New Mexico, by Indians, Anglos, and Hispanics alike. During those years, New Mexico remained a poor, rather backward state, remote from national life, with an ethnographic, economic, and social makeup unlike any other state. According to a 1934 article in the *American Mercury* in 1934: "[New Mexico] has remained

behind the walls of the Rockies, a state *in* but not *of* the United States."

Because of the state's seeming inability to govern itself during the twenties, Republican Senator Bronson Cutting had argued for *more* federal government, believing that to be the only social institution that could ensure opportunities for his constituents. An editorial in his Santa Fe *New Mexican* proposed, only half in jest, that the state legislature be abolished because it could not handle the increasing demands on it for services.

By 1930, New Mexico remained a chaotic tangle of diverse ethnic groups who could not agree on policies or programs to help them solve common problems of land and water use, unemployment, health, or education. The illiteracy rate in New Mexico was 15.9 percent in 1930, compared with 6 percent nationwide. Poverty affected more than 40 percent of the population, a condition that was more pronounced among those who tried to scratch a living from the eroded land along the Rio Grande and its tribu-

Above: Rehabilitation clients. Mexican jacal on the left in which they formerly lived and the new house built with a Resettlement Administration loan. Doña Ana County, 1936. Arthur Rothstein.
LC-USF 34-2910-D

Right: A Spanish-American rancher. Chacon, 1943. John Collier, Jr.
LC-USW 3-15281-C

taries. In that area, the predominantly Spanish-speaking population subsisted on less than $100 a year.

More than a half century of Anglo exploitation had resulted in a drastically decreased land base for native Hispanics. During the thirties, New Mexico was little more than a feudal state, economically and politically controlled by Anglos who often reduced their Hispanic neighbors to dependent positions that amounted to servitude. Ethnic and economic lines were clearly drawn. Enormous and frequently violent rifts existed between the land barons and those living in abject poverty, between eastern cattlemen and the oil field workers, and between property owners and a steady influx of migrants pouring in from Texas, Oklahoma, and the Midwest. Historian William Pickens, author of *The New Deal in New*

Mexico, described life in the thirties as follows:

> One economic bottom gave way to another, and the public sank into common despair. Perhaps the most frightening part of these days was that people could turn to no one. The barons were powerless and silent. Large landowners, men respected throughout the state, offered little advice except sentences punctuated with a rifle when indigents invaded their property. The few powerful businessmen in New Mexico were crushed and hopeless; some of their counterparts in the East called for a dictatorship. Left without institutional leadership, small communities were drawn together as never before. Many experienced demonstrations such as the day twenty cars jammed with veterans en route to the Bonus March "invaded Raton." Some damage was done, but citizens paid them little mind. The town gave them food, shelter, entertainment, road maps, and best wishes.
>
> State government touched the lives of few people. Officials in Santa Fe simply ceased to plan programs. Tax collection was sporadic and usually resisted. Many departments did little except draw up budgets. The government in Santa Fe sat, much like the giant corporations in America, waiting for some kind of change. Even for agrarian New Mexico, the end had been reached in early 1933. One-third of all New Mexicans required some governmental relief to approach subsistence living when Franklin D. Roosevelt became the thirty-second president.

The election of 1932 marked the beginning of the shift away from the old guard Republicanism that had controlled New Mexico throughout the 1920s. An impoverished populace listened to Roosevelt's campaign promise to lift them out of their misery; at the same time a powerful Democratic machine penetrated into rural areas, promising relief. The strategy worked. An unprecedented 80 percent of New Mexico's eligible voters cast their ballots in 1932, and Roosevelt carried the state by 63.7 percent of the vote. All statewide offices were captured by Democrats, but no state program or ideology emerged.

No sooner had Roosevelt announced his New Deal programs than hundreds of millions of federal dollars poured into New Mexico to fund everything from schools to day care centers, welfare payments to relief work. Zealous New Dealers swept into Santa Fe with bureaus, application forms, and reams of regulations. Few politicians at the local level knew how to cope with the overwhelming array of red tape and bureaucracy; some programs crashed because no one knew how to run them; others yielded to the old patronage system. In *Politics in New Mexico,* Jack Holmes

charged that "highway department maintenance crews were under the patronage of county chairmen, and several of the more enterprising of the local party functionaries acquired equipment which they then leased or rented to the department." However, patronage or not, the state highway department, with an annual budget of $5 million, managed to construct almost 500 miles of highways per year, second only to Colorado in the Rocky Mountain West.

In 1934, nearly 12,000 people were employed by the Civil Works Administration, but a survey revealed that as many as half of these people did no work at all. By mid-1935, 28 percent of all New Mexicans were on relief, the highest in the nation. Around $75 million in federal dollars flowed in each year for the duration of the depression, earmarked for the construction of dams, schoolhouses, roads, and bridges. At the state and local levels, the budget rose to a record $24 million in fiscal 1932, yet New Mexico's standard of living did not improve significantly until after World War II.

As new programs mushroomed virtually overnight, politics became the tool by which to secure a job. One drought-irrigation project went from 1,300 employees to 5,200 in five days. Other federal projects came to a standstill, often because regulations did not provide tools or equipment to complete them. Only the Child Welfare Service, which in April 1938 had 17,949 cases and spent $106,073 for indigents, remained free of the scandal that tainted other agencies.

Left: Rehabilitation client and a stallion purchased through a rehabilitation loan. Doña Ana County, 1936. Arthur Rothstein. LC-USF 34-2860-E

Right: Threshing wheat. Questa, 1939. Russell Lee. LC-USF 34-34313-D

Graft soon entered the reality of the New Deal in New Mexico. In order to keep their jobs, state workers were expected to kick back a portion of their earnings to the local political machine. According to Jack Holmes, 6,484 state workers, with the exception of teachers, professors, and those covered by the Hatch Act (prohibiting government employees from engaging in political activity), were subject to a political levy upon their paychecks. Holmes claims that such payoffs amounted to at least $40,000 a year statewide, reason enough during the depression to make party control worth the effort. To make matters worse, Holmes observed that between 1935 and 1940, "one could normally find on the roster of state officers and employees [of the federal pro-grams] from a third to a half of the county chairmen." The corruption of the public works program eventually resulted in a grand jury indictment of seventy-three employees, including the former WPA administrator in New Mexico; only five were actually convicted.

Five years into the New Deal, some appalling statistics indicated that federal programs had not improved the basic quality of life in New Mexico at all. The illiteracy rate remained at 15 percent; malnutrition and infant mortality were 30 percent higher than the rest of the country. Per capita income remained two-thirds of the national average. Total cash receipts from farming were slightly over $50 million, down $18 million from 1929, considered the last good year for

agriculture before the drought cycle began. Oil, tourists, and federal employment kept the state on its feet economically during the depression years as agriculture and mining revenues plunged.

Only cotton farmers, the main target of the Agricultural Adjustment Administration, benefited substantially from federal largesse: in 1933, 1,600 cotton farmers received $700,000 for plowing up one-fourth of their total acreage to prevent a market glut. Federal controls, along with widespread drought, actually more than doubled the price of cotton between 1934 and 1935, creating a short-lived prosperity for cotton farmers.

Other farmers were not as fortunate. As the bottom fell out of the wheat, corn, and hog markets, hundreds of farmers declared bankruptcy. Others signed up for AAA programs, hoping that federal funds would save them. However, in agriculturally based Curry County, AAA contracts provided only 10 percent of income for farmers who had signed up. In the face of continuing low prices, one bureaucrat cheerfully concluded:

"One of the most important accomplishments of the AAA in New Mexico has been to show farmers how to organize and work together."

But organization was the furthest thing from most farmers' minds. By this time, the average value of New Mexico farmland was about $4 an acre, one-eighth of the national average. Many farmers, faced with federal loans they couldn't pay, walked off and left everything—plows, furniture, and livestock included.

Nor were farmers the only ones hit. Between 1937 and 1938, urban employment fell by 17 percent. Mining income had dropped to $6 million a year. In 1933 more than 8,000 New Mexico children were not receiving an education because their schools had shut down for lack of funds. By that time, 50 percent of the banks had failed, including the state's largest, the First National Bank of Albuquerque. People were hungry, and they roamed the streets, scouring garbage pails, begging nickels from passersby. In 1935, an angry crowd of out-of-work men stormed the county welfare office in Albuquerque, demanding aid. The terrified administrator,

one E. N. Boule, fled through the window when the mob battered down his door.

In 1935, a government team was sent from Washington to investigate the deplorable conditions in northern New Mexican villages. Their report—called the Tewa Basin Study—stated that the 20,000 residents of Hispanic villages of the Upper Rio Grande Valley suffered acutely during this time. Up to 1929, the report said, on the average of one person per family went out to work four to seven months of the year, at wages varying from $40 to $100 a month. Because of the depression, these jobs were no longer available during the thirties; only two or three men from communities worked outside, compared to 100–150 a decade earlier. The report concluded: "The net result is that at the present time the relief load is between 60 and 70 percent of the people of the area, and most of the people not receiving relief are indirectly depending for a livelihood upon relief orders."

The failure of the New Deal in Hispanic villages was also due to the fact that bureaucrats, reams of forms and regulations in hand, swept in from Washington, ignoring local agricultural

agents who had managed to form a fragile link between villagers and the bureaucracy. The newcomers spoke no Spanish; few villagers spoke English. The result was that, except for direct emergency relief, little attempt was made to discover the roots of Hispanic misery, or to educate the Hispanic people in matters of food production, job training, or health. So great was the bitterness toward all things federal that in rural Hispanic New Mexico the WPA became known as "el diablo a pie"—the devil on foot. Yet federal aid soon became part of everyday life, a pattern that exists to the present day in the form of food stamps, welfare payments, and commodities.

While few Hispanic villages were able to pull themselves out of the depression, one public works project succeeded through the sheer effort of the people involved. The Taos County Project, initially funded by private sources as well as by the University of New Mexico, was a successful experiment in cooperative county planning and action. Between 1940 and 1943, hundreds of local Hispanic residents took responsibility to work on deep-seated problems that had been present for generations. They did it because,

Above: Wagons are the only form of transportation for most of the Hispanic people served by the Taos County Cooperative Health Association. This family has driven through a snowstorm to bring a sick baby to the clinic. Peñasco, 1943. John Collier, Jr. LC-USW 3-18047-C

Right: The waiting room of the clinic. Health care was poor prior to the 1940s. Peñasco, 1943. John Collier, Jr. LC-USW 3-13655-C

according to Blas Chávez of Los Cordovas, "We did not want people to think we were lazy. We wanted to do as our fathers and grandfathers taught us."

From the small communities surrounding Taos, representatives gathered to share their problems and to explore ways to resolve them. Some communities wanted practical things: community water wells, electricity, erosion control, a hot lunch program, roads, playgrounds, and a community center. Others asked for the next-to-impossible: to get land back taken away by the Picuris Indians, to lower taxes, and to retain their original land grants, by then out of their hands for more than half a century.

One significant result of this project was a county library system, consisting of eleven branch libraries in communities which had never had them before. The project also included a bookmobile, the first in the state. It was a crude affair, a one-and-a-half-ton truck chassis with a school bus minus the windows. Nonetheless, it held 800 books, many of them written in Spanish, and a Spanish edition of the *Reader's Digest*. So popular was the bookmobile in these isolated communities that, when winter snows precluded its arrival in Amalia, a local man solved the dilemma. He simply saddled his horse, loaded his saddlebags with books, and took them from house to house, checking them out to villagers in good library style. The "book-horse" went where the bookmobile could not go.

A collection of films, none of which really addressed the indigenous problems, was shown throughout small Hispanic communities in Taos County. Many residents who had never seen a film before walked up to three miles each way, young children in their arms, to the churches or community centers to see films like "Building the Boulder Dam," "Farm Inconveniences," "Frontiers of the Future," and "Stop Forest Fires." In one year, 1941–42, a record 52,745 people turned up.

In Cerro, the community went one step further when it organized to overhaul the ancient acequia system, providing the labor, wagons and teams, and necessary materials such as logs, sand, and gravel themselves. A small grant from the Soil Conservation Service paid for commercial materials when the FSA refused, but the community provided the rest. When the job was complete, the flow of water had been increased by some 50 percent.

Other improvements involving the Taos County Project included soil erosion control, tax reform, a school lunch program, handicraft training, and the Taos County Cooperative Health Association. While New Deal monies were used to fund major projects such as the health cooperative, no federal funds were spent on soil erosion control or the tax reform package. Local people, after having a major share in planning the county program, decided against WPA work projects and assumed the responsibility for local materials and labor themselves.

The Taos County Project was an anomaly in the midst of the graft, corruption, and mismanagement of New Deal programs. New Mexico remained out of the mainstream of American life, and partly because of its remoteness and political naïveté federal officials chose the isolated site of Los Alamos for the research and development of the atomic bomb in the early 1940s. The state slumbered on. Not until after World War II would economic development really begin, and then on the frequently erratic course of previous years. As territorial governor Lew Wallace once observed: "Every calculation based on experience elsewhere fails in New Mexico."

Even today, many state residents might agree.

Right: A dentist making an extraction at the health clinic. Peñasco, 1943. John Collier, Jr.
LC-USW 3-17898-C

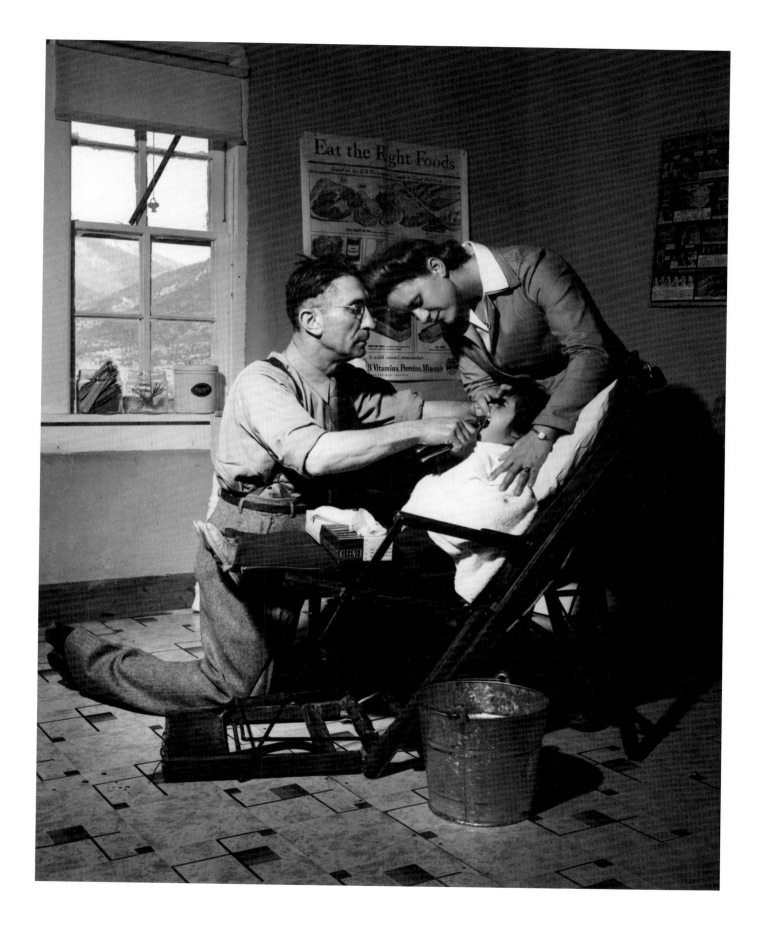

CHAPTER ONE

DUST BOWL & RESETTLEMENT

When the dust storms came, I thought the world was coming to an end. The chickens went to roost at noon. We had to light the lamps in the middle of the day. They closed the schools. When I got home, I'd sweep dust and cry, sweep dust and cry. One time I swept five pounds from the kitchen table.

Mildred Welch, Springer, about her life in New Mexico's Dust Bowl

If we was lucky, we made twelve dollars a week. You could live on that, if you could grow a little food, have chickens, a cow or two, a hog. But after a while the dust choked everything to death, the garden, the wheat, the corn, the cows even. So there was nuthin' left, not even a row of beans. You wanted to leave, but there was nowhere to go. You wanted to work, but there was three men for every job.

Milton Horn, Springer, about his life in Mills, New Mexico

Hell is a beautiful name for what we went through.

Albert Bada, Dust Bowl farmer, Gladstone, New Mexico

Opposite: Resettled farm child from Taos Junction, a government rehabilitation community that failed to take hold. Bosque Farms, 1935. Dorothea Lange.
LC-USF 34-1638-E

The Dust Bowl is a loosely defined geographic area that includes eastern New Mexico, eastern Colorado, western Kansas, western Oklahoma, and the Texas Panhandle. It is a vast, windswept land, covering more than 100 million acres, largely empty of detail except for a windmill here and there, a lone cottonwood along a twisted arroyo filled with sand, a barbed wire fence stretching toward the horizon, or a solitary homestead crumbling back into the earth. The blistering heat of summer, the fierce blizzards of winter, the unrelenting winds that drove so many pioneer women crazy are stark components of an inhospitable land —and testimony to the strength of the people who survived the depression.

The Dust Bowl has its own peculiar landscape; it is a diary of hundreds of millions of years of geologic change ranging from primordial mountains wearing away long ago, to successive advances and retreats of seas over a newly made continent, and to the last retreat of the seas and the emergence of the land. Dinosaurs once lumbered across the marshlands of what is now Union County; 10,000 years ago prehistoric Folsom man hunted giant bison with spears near the New Mexico town for which he is named. As millennia passed, the climate changed; a sea of tall grass spread from horizon to horizon. Great herds of smaller bison (buffalo) moved across the endless expanse, tracked by Indians carrying bows and arrows.

Across this landscape, where the sky presses down in relentless monotony and the wind tears at mind and body, the fur trappers, the gold seekers, and the settlers hurried to someplace else—to the high valleys and mountains farther west. Only one group of men thought that this hostile landscape had any value at all. In 1877, while the Indians and the buffalo still inhabited the land, cattlemen began driving huge herds down from the Colorado gold camps and up from southern Texas. As many as ten million head of cattle chewed the once-plentiful grasses down to a stubble. What had taken thousands of years to build up was destroyed before the end of the century. Cattlemen soon moved westward to virgin pastures.

Sodbusters streamed onto the plains of eastern New Mexico in the wake of the cattle boom. Some settled where the cattle had been; others filed claims under the provisions of the Homestead Act of 1862. By this time, all that was left was the barren land shunned even by the cattlemen who correctly perceived that the elements would eventually win. Many sodbusters gave up and moved on, some back to the midwestern states from which they'd come, others to a western frontier that beckoned with what appeared to be limitless opportunity to "prove up." It was clear, as many believed, that "there ain't no God west of Salina."

The cattlemen, by this time having worn out the land to which they'd moved two decades earlier, moved back, buying up relinquishments from one farm family after another. In the plains of New Mexico, an estimated one million acres were claimed by cattlemen who began to build huge empires, many of which survive to the present day. Other farmers arrived from the Midwest, unpacked their wagons, and began the task of taming the land, just as the generation before them had done. They made the same mistakes, plowing up the fragile grassland and trying to plant wheat, corn, beans, and sorghums which disturbed the thin layer of ground cover. By 1920, signs of erosion had already begun.

"The thing that made the land blow away wasn't wheat, it was pinto beans," says Jess Jordan, son of a Dust Bowl farmer who lost his homestead near Mills during the depression. "When you harvest pinto beans, you go right down into the ground. There's no stubble left, nothing to hold down the ground. It just up and blew away."

Jess Jordan's father and mother came to New Mexico from Missouri in 1914, riding in an "immigrant train," a rented railroad boxcar that also contained their three children, a wagon, and two horses. They unloaded at Roy and staked a claim on 360 acres five miles east of Mills, an area settled around the turn of the century by wheat farmers from Texas, Oklahoma, and Kansas. The Jordans, like other homesteaders of their time, soon realized that it would take 10,000

Opposite: Fence corner and out-building being buried by dust. Long years of land abuse have resulted in conditions such as this. Mills, 1935. Dorothea Lange.

acres to make a living. Dependent upon nature for their survival, they pushed the land to its limit, year after year. Finally, the land gave up; coincidentally, a cycle of drought began.

For two or three years, there was no rain. The heat broke all records, reaching 115 degrees in eastern New Mexico in 1934; the earth cracked open, corn fields sizzled, grasshoppers came and ate everything, including fence posts, laundry, and vegetable gardens. WPA workers spread as much as 60,000 pounds of poison a day in an effort to salvage what crops were left. One farmer, after counting the dead grasshoppers under five watermelons, reported that the insect population, if evenly distributed, would equal 23,400 grasshoppers per acre. In Union County, the work of the grasshopper brigade was temporarily halted when five separate flights of grasshoppers flew over Clayton as the insects migrated from Colorado and Oklahoma. Workers sought cover from the thick pall of insects that filled the sky much the same as the dust storms of the time.

Throughout New Mexico's eastern plains, second- and third-generation homesteaders began to feel a new unease as they watched their life's work fall to ruin. Cattle lay dead along fence lines where the dust began to pile up. There was no money and no credit. The banks, in fact, were closed. Farm workers, once hired by the dozen, stood by, victims of the plow. Many farmers, remembering the prosperity of only a few years before, refused to give up hope.

"Even in the worst of it, 1934 or 5, we thought we'd still pull out," says Franklin Welch, whose mother cooked for the Wilson Mercantile Company's hotel in Mills while his father was a janitor at the local school. "Nobody wanted to believe we never would survive. It was the dust, you see, that got us in the end."

When the great blizzards began to roll across the plains in 1933, one-third of the Dust Bowl region, including most of eastern New Mexico, lay naked and vulnerable. As the land slid away into the creek bottoms, a fine mist of dust seeped through the windows of flimsy farmhouses that were sometimes made of nothing more than tar paper and boards.

"We didn't know from one day to the next what would happen," says Mildred Welch, a Texas sharecropper's daughter whose father, Lon Madole, homesteaded near Mills. To help make ends meet he set up a barbershop in his home, charging twenty-five cents for a haircut and fifteen cents for a shave. Now living in Springer

with her husband, Franklin, Mildred Welch has clear memories of the Dust Bowl days.

> Sometimes there would be a little rain. Then dust. Then more dust. The static electricity was so bad, it'd kill the ignition if you were out driving somewhere. I remember one day, my mom and dad and us kids was drivin' back from town in the truck. A dust storm came up and dad tried to beat it home. A mile or so from the house, the engine quit. Dad was afraid to wait it out so we started for the house. The sand whipped my legs somethin' fierce. Mother was afraid the baby would suffocate, so she wrapped his head in a blanket. We couldn't see a thing. The only way we got home was to follow the fence line along.

Even then, the Madole family thought that better times would come again to Harding County where they had tried so hard to make a living.

But the boom days were already over. In 1929, the year that the stock market crashed and the rest of the country was plunged into a depression, most of Harding and Union counties were riding on an economic crest solely based on agriculture. During prohibition, Union County had reaped its first bonanza when it became a major producer of moonshine for the Dallas and Denver trade. Until 1930, rainfall had been plentiful, more than seventeen inches that year alone. Bumper crops were harvested, but then the rains stopped. No cash crops were harvested for two, three, and four years in a row. Most farmers, living on a shoestring, could not even afford to pay the interest on notes amounting to $100 or less. Banks foreclosed on farms and repossessed the very machines that had brought such devastation to the land. "We could have survived the depression," says Jess Jordan who found work during the 1930s with the WPA, "if it hadn't been for the drought."

In Dust Bowl country, something is always to blame other than the men who made it happen. Pinto beans. Drought. Depression. The land itself which yielded to the plow, then "went sour on us." The dry, scrubby earth of Harding County, where the Jordans and hundreds of other families homesteaded in the early 1900s, was never fit for farming to begin with. Except for the Canadian River on the western boundary of the county, there is little natural running water to provide irrigation. Rainfall averages less than ten inches per year; the soil is dry, coarse, and nutrient-poor.

"If God had meant anything to grow in Harding County," said one old Dust Bowl farmer, "He would have given us trees." Another, watching

his former cropland blow away, quipped, "Reckon I'll have to sue Kansas to git it back." In nearby farmhouses, women rushed to lay wet towels around windows to keep out the dust. Lines were strung between outhouses and front doorknobs so people would not get lost. One woman placed food *under* a tablecloth during dust storms, and each family member, once seated, would raise his corner of the cloth and begin eating. A paralyzing fear set in.

By May 1934, 350 million tons of dust were airborne. Dust storms, like those experienced by Mildred Welch and her family, seemed never-ending. An exasperated Plains woman wrote in her journal, "This is the ultimate darkness. So must come the end of the world." Upright, hard-working, and honest, the Dust Bowl people believed that the dust storms were evidence of an apocalyptic vengeance let loose by a spiteful God. An elderly wheat farmer from Roy, who requested that his name not be used, said, "Me and the wife was church-goin', God-fearin' people till '35. When the dust come, it was like we had done somethin' wrong. Lost everything, even the dog. We got down and prayed, day after day. But it didn't do no good. God didn't answer nobody's prayers in Harding County that year."

When Dorothea Lange arrived in Harding County in the spring of 1935, the land was already "tractored out." More than 72,000 acres had been repossessed, most of it worthless land. Hundreds of families had left, some swept up into the vast migration west, others to jobs in town, still others to government rehabilitation projects. Bosque Farms near Albuquerque and Agua Fria in Arizona were federally designed communities where they hoped to start over once again. Lange took pictures of the Dust Bowl around Mills, even getting caught in a black blizzard herself as she snapped away on farm after devastated farm. She spoke to residents about their stubborn hopes to press yet another crop from the worn-out land.

One weary farmer, still plowing through the dust with his young son, said to her, "I left cotton growing east of Wichita Falls to come out here to grow wheat. I guess I've made 1,000 miles right up and down this field in the dust when you couldn't see that car on the road. And I've had to use headlights in the middle of the day when it was so dark you couldn't see your hand in front of your face."

When Lange was there, Mills was still a company town, owned by the Wilson Mercantile Company, which also owned a hotel, the grocery

store, the grain elevator, and the mill. There was also a bank, a school, a drugstore where the pharmacist pulled teeth in a back room, three doctors, two saloons, a theatre where shows came all the way from Albuquerque, a ten-by-ten-foot jail, two lumber yards, two more hotels, and the "Sufferin' Pacific" railroad which ran two trains a day between Tucumcari and a coal mine at nearby Dawson.

For a number of years, in a long-held rural American tradition, the Wilson Company let local farmers buy on credit for a whole year until harvest, then they would be paid out of the farmers' proceeds. As conditions worsened, there were no proceeds. The struggling flour company repossessed thousands of acres put up for collat-

Above: Wife and child who are clients for resettlement. Mills, 1935. Dorothea Lange. LC-USF 34-1629-E

Right: A Resettlement Administration land use project. This family is to be resettled, their land to revert to cattle range even though there is little remaining grass. Mills, 1935. Dorothea Lange. LC-USF 34-1634-E

eral but could not sell them. By 1940, the Wilson Company had gone bankrupt itself; all that remained in Mills were the post office and a grocery store. Only a handful of people hung on.

Bobby Dennis and his wife, Peggy, are the last residents of Mills, living in a little house on top of a hill from which they can see for miles around. Most of the buildings photographed by Lange in 1935 are gone, the railroad bed is simply a soft rise in the bleached-out land, and all of the houses are boarded up. The post office is where the grocery store used to be, and Bobby Dennis owns it. In fact, he owns most of the town.

"I been here for fifty-two years," he says, stopping his pickup long enough to chat in the middle of Mills's dusty, deserted main street. He has a weathered look and a matter-of-fact way of speaking. "Don't reckon I'll go anyplace else." He is a stout, ruddy-faced man, who wears a pair of tiny dark glasses with lenses the size of fifty-cent pieces.

His wife, Peggy, small, shy, and reluctant to speak very many words at a time, looks away to the east where the dust storms used to blot out the sun. She came here from Plainview, Texas, with her family in 1929. Her father used to be a sharecropper and he tried to plant wheat here, but he was "blowed-out, like the rest of 'em." Times were hard for this family, too, and Peggy Dennis, barely twenty years old then, learned something from the experience. "When you've

been through the Dust Bowl, you don't expect too much," she says. Her life has been simple, filled with family, friends, and hard work. She never expected more.

Married to Bobby in 1944, Peggy Dennis became postmistress the same year, a job she held until 1980. She was the human link between far-flung neighbors in the sprawling country around Mills. She was always the first to know about births and deaths and marriages, and sometimes she gave advice to those who came to fetch their mail.

"There's something here," she says fondly, looking at the boarded-up houses as if they still housed her old friends. "You can go away, then you come back and you're satisfied." She does not

see the choking stillness of the town nor is she aware that she is in the midst of its final decay. Peggy Dennis sees what she wants to see.

Bobby Dennis was twenty-two years old in 1935, when he came to Mills from Kansas with his family. His father worked for years at the flour mill and his mother took in boarders; nine of them crammed at one time into a small white frame house that still stands in an overgrown field across from the post office. Bobby went to work before he was twelve, herding cattle for fifty cents a day; he had to ride bareback because he couldn't afford a saddle. He went on to counting eggs at the company store, then "graduated" to the creamery, then finally to the beanery where he cleaned, sacked, and loaded pinto beans

Left: Discouraged farmers have been leaving this area over a period of years, leaving their heavy equipment in the fields. Mills, 1934. Dorothea Lange. LC-USF 34-2767-E

Right: By the time Dorothea Lange reached Mills in May 1935, the grain elevator in the background was already abandoned. Because of a high rate of foreclosures, the bank had failed the year before. The Wilson Company store and hotel, right, closed in 1940. LC-USF 34-1627-E

onto boxcars. He got $1.25 a day, which he considered good wages. In 1941, after everything closed, he opened his own grocery and ran it until 1952. He says he never made much money, but "we made a livin' and were mighty glad at that. We can't expect to get rich in this life. A place to sleep and enough to eat." Like his wife, Bobby does not admit that Mills is almost a ghost town, kept alive only by their presence. He is proud to be the last survivor, proud of his ability to recite the town's short history, but more important, he knows he is the only direct link to a time that is receding into a gradually dimming past.

During the Dust Bowl days, Bobby Dennis worked extra hours to hang on his small homestead near town where he and his father ran a few cattle, but as the grass began to die, there was nothing left to feed them. "So these government boys came in and shot my whole herd. What took us ten years to build up they destroyed in one day. But we was so much in debt we couldn't afford to feed 'em, just watched 'em get thinner and thinner. I guess they must have shot about fifty cows and calves. Paid twelve dollars for a cow, two dollars for a calf." However, the Dennises, like thousands of other Dust Bowl farmers who lost their cattle, received none of this money; it was owed to the Federal Land Bank and other lending agencies, such as the Wilson Company. Furthermore, according to government regulations, the owner was allowed to keep only enough of the slaughtered cattle to feed his family; the rest were to be dragged away and left to rot. "It was the only time in my life I ever broke the law," confesses Bobby Dennis. "I stood there lookin' at all those dead cattle and I got in my truck and drove all over the country telling people where they could find meat. By morning it was all gone." With a certain sense of satisfaction, Bobby Dennis drives off, a cloud of dust rising behind his pickup.

In the Dust Bowl states, many others like Bobby Dennis resolved to stay, even as the insidious dust was turning their property into a wasteland. It was drought, and drought alone, they believed, that caused the Dust Bowl. "When the rains return," "when the drought quits," "if we can just hang on" became the rallying cries of a stubborn group of plainspeople who refused to quit. They are still to be found on their inhospitable land, having wrung a living from it all these years.

One of these survivors is Albert Bada who, with his parents and seven brothers and sisters,

settled on a homestead a few miles northeast of Mills in 1915, just three years after New Mexico became a state. Albert Bada was then seven years old. He remembers the transportation of those days—a wagon train consisting of five horse-drawn wagons that went from Shamrock, Texas, to the wilds of eastern New Mexico. The 250-mile trip took three weeks. Once they arrived at their 320-acre homestead, the Bada children slept in the covered wagon until fall and their parents stayed in a crude eight-by-ten-foot shack made of tar paper and boards. A dugout eventually served as a bedroom for the children; the dirt-floored, one-room shack was gradually expanded to include several rooms. The Bada family could not afford a wood-frame home for twelve years. Bit by bit, the family added to their land, a few hundred acres at a time, growing crops of pinto beans, corn, oats, and wheat. They also raised cows, hogs, and chickens.

"We borrowed, bought a little land, and hoped to God we could pay for it. Us boys all worked for Dad. Every dollar I made went into his pocket until I was twenty-one years old," says the old homesteader, a huge man with enormous, well-worn hands. He lives today not far from where his family originally settled, on a 5,000-acre spread he calls the Sugar Loaf Ranch.

Family devotion and cooperation enabled the Badas to survive thirty years of hardship. The elder Mr. Bada, originally from Czechoslovakia, knew the value of husbanding the soil, so he did not push his land to its limit, according to his son. Albert Bada insists that they could have continued to raise good crops all during the Dust

Above: Tarpaper shacks were typical homesteader dwellings in the Mills area during the thirties. Dugouts like the one on the left provided shelter while the tarpaper homes were being built. Mills, 1935. Dorothea Lange.
LC-USF 34-2766-E

Right: The mass migration out of the Dust Bowl to California began in 1935. Here three related drought refugee families are stalled on the highway near Lordsburg, 1937. Dorothea Lange.
LC-USF 34-16676-C

Bowl years but, "what come in blew in from neighbors' places, here and over yonder." They always managed to find something to eat, despite the harsh conditions. "We'd go out and there'd be a little stalk of corn stickin' out of the sand. We'd grab an ear or two, shuck it, and make it into mush. Sometimes, down in a draw, we'd find a whole row. The same with wheat. You'd find a little patch that the dust hadn't kilt, so you'd harvest that, thresh it, grind it up. Mama would have enough flour for ten, twenty loaves of bread."

Like the Dennises in Mills, the Badas lost their cattle, but were allowed to keep their chickens and sold the eggs for six cents a dozen. With that money, Mrs. Bada bought fabric and made clothing for her family. "Shoes we handed down. I'd wear Dad's old shoes even though they was a couple of sizes too big and hold 'em on with balin' wire. It was that or go barefoot. I remember at Christmas us eight kids would gather round and sing songs, we didn't expect no presents. If Mama bought me a pair of socks, I figured I was livin' in heaven."

Hard work, frugality, and a will to survive kept the Bada family on the land, year after year. Today, Albert Bada and his brothers own 10,000 acres in Harding County, free and clear. "I'll tell you how we made it when others just give up. If we didn't raise it, we did without. It was as simple as that."

To help people like the Badas, New Dealers in 1934 passed legislation that provided emergency feed loans and permitted government acquisition of submarginal lands and the relocation of Dust Bowl families. The Taylor Grazing Act of 1934, a complex and far-reaching law, was written to make cattlemen responsible for their own mistakes, including the overgrazing that had decimated millions of acres of federal land used by them for half a century. When cattlemen balked at placing restrictions on themselves, millions of acres of western rangelands were placed under the control of the BLM (Bureau of Land Manage-

ment). The federal agency withdrew virtually all land from further homesteading, making it impossible for families to acquire free land like the Badas had. It was the end of an era. In addition, the Soil Conservation Act, passed in 1935, paid farmers to retire their ruined land and put it into the soil bank. The check, of course, went to the owner of the land. This law had the unfortunate consequence of dispossessing the tenant farmers and sharecroppers of the Dust Bowl and turning them into migrants. Millions of dollars more were allocated to curb the blowing soil, in effect paying those farmers who decided to stay for working their own land.

Bureaucrats, when confronted by destitute farmers pleading for more money, pointed out that federal subsidies were never meant to do more than show farmers how to organize and work together. The irony was that most farmers were too exhausted, broke, and depressed to consider more than day-to-day survival. As Albert Bada put it, "Most of the (federal) programs was a joke. We didn't want to hear about none of 'em. The fellers that signed up, well, they're the ones that went away."

Opposite and below: An Iowa family of eleven, stranded and penniless in southeastern New Mexico, August 1936.
LC-USF 34-9750-E
LC-USF 34-9747-E

By 1934, after a year's futile fight against the desolation and the black winds, refugees from America's Sahara began moving westward in ancient jalopies; some even went on foot, dragging their belongings in carts. Cars and trucks were piled high with torn mattresses, cooking utensils, and miscellaneous possessions from their homesteads and farms "back east." On the running boards were strapped cages with live goats, chickens, and pigs in them. "Goin' down the road feelin' bad," sang Woody Guthrie. Tens of thousands agreed.

At the height of the exodus, as many as 20,000 homeless people jammed the roads. So many left Oklahoma that the name "Okie" was applied to all the migrants regardless of where they were from. Thousands of displaced families drove nearly bumper to bumper westward through Idaho on U.S. 30, or across New Mexico and Arizona following Route 66, or on the old Spanish Trail through El Paso. Dorothea Lange captured images of grimy children peering out from behind the junk, gaunt, sad-eyed women nursing their babies, and tubercular men stranded along the road. These exhausted men carried with them memories of their failures and the slim hope of finding a new life in the promised land of California. Lange wrote in her notebook her impressions of one migrant family stranded near Lordsburg, "Left Iowa in 1932 because of father's ill health. Father was an auto mechanic, laborer, painter by trade—tubercular. Nine children including a sick four-month-old baby. No money at all. About to sell their belongings and truck for money to buy food. 'We don't want to go where we'll be a nuisance to anybody.'"

In 1935, government statistics showed that across the nation, fifteen million Americans were out of work; over a million women and children were deserted by jobless men. The great westward migration began when the federal government began its program of turning the Dust Bowl back to grassland under the provisions of the Soil Conservation Act. To achieve that end, the government announced plans to move 100,000 families out of the Dust Bowl into resettlement areas, a notion that outraged farmers determined to stay.

Others, however, listened to federal agricultural agents, signed the necessary papers, and moved away, never to return to their lands. The government paid between two and five dollars an acre for these lands even though the Department of Agriculture valued some areas ten times higher. Other farmers were forced out when the Federal Land Bank would not renew their loans, some of them for as little as eighty dollars. Still others were enticed by government brochures sent out to those farmers living in areas about to be bought, telling them that they could trade their poor, overworked farms for good croplands, varying in size from twenty-five to one hundred acres, "with good buildings and other excellent preparations for farming."

The brochures hinted at an abundant water supply, rich soil, good homes with running water, electricity, fences, and roads. There was no mention that the already bankrupt farmer would have to pay for these things himself. However, another government publication, aimed at county agents in the field, warned that farmers might not be able to make a living from farming, but might have to find part-time work in "nearby forests, parks, or grazing districts [or] on farms operated by more capable individuals. . . ."

The strategy worked. During this time, the Dust Bowl states suffered an alarming exodus. Almost a million Plains people left their farms in the first half of the decade, and 2.5 million left after 1935, not all of them "dusted out" but uprooted by government promises, through New Deal programs, to help them survive. In these cases, survival was on the terms of the federal government. Statistics from the Department of Agriculture show that 10,000 homes stood abandoned on the high plains; nine million acres of farmland were turned back to nature, bought up, and eventually resold by the government. It is not clear where the uprooted people went.

Under terms set forth by the Resettlement Administration (later known as the Farm Security Administration), Dust Bowl farmers agreed to sell their drought-stricken land and to be settled on "good land" chosen by the Resettlement Administration. Officially, according to Department of Agriculture procedures, the FSA photographers were to document the relocation process in three stages: first, to show the destitute farmer on his worn-out land; second, to show him happily resettled on a government farm; and third, to show the bureaucracy at work to keep the farmer content in his new surroundings. Photographs of bureaucrats, FSA clients, dams, road projects, land reclamation, and successful crop production were requested by Roy Stryker's superiors to raise support for New Deal programs, which in turn kept the Historical Section alive. But by Stryker's own admission he "bootlegged" into the

collection as many as 40,000 negatives of ordinary lives. "I wanted to know who the American people were and what they were going through," he said in a 1972 interview.

Destitute farmers and their families moved onto individual tracts of thirty acres or less and soon found that they were required to do all the development work, including building fences, roads, and houses. The labor costs for these improvements were to be debited to the rehabilitation project and included in the price of the land paid by the settlers. The federal government kept all water rights and charged the resettlement families a fee for the water.

Dust Bowl farmers soon realized that they had traded an improved homestead of at least 160 acres for 30 acres of unimproved land, and they did not even own the water rights. Moreover, the

Right: A Dust Bowl farmer plows his field with a hitch tractor, near Mills, 1938. Dorothea Lange.
LC-USF 34-18267-C

Below: A young boy, stranded with his family near Lordsburg, 1935. Dorothea Lange.
LC-USF 34-9752-C

government laid down certain guidelines to what it called its "business partners." A 1934 bulletin from the Resettlement Administration said that the government would help

> plan gardens which will meet the family's needs; determine what quantity and kinds of foods are needed to supply the family's dietary needs; determine what food may be utilized during the growing season and what food may be processed for use during the winter months; plan the family's clothing budget, including an analysis of old clothing that may be utilized for wear or to make rugs, etc.

In addition, the government's "family manage-ment plan" included a list of who would do which family chores such as washing dishes, milking the cows, feeding the chickens, and mending the fences. The government also decided what furniture a family could buy and what kinds of fuel were allowed to heat their homes.

The situation was not the promised utopia, but a form of slavery, with individuals forfeited to the bureaucracy. Farmers could not even do what they did best and often took menial jobs as agricultural workers or went to surrounding towns and tried to find work, just as the govern-ment brochure had predicted a few years earlier.

Opposite: Government rehabilitation farms offered a way for some Dust Bowl refugees to start over. Here a man begins to level a tract of 2,400 acres with a team and fresno in order to cultivate the land for dairy farming. Thousands of huge cottonwood trees like those in the background were dug out, using horses. Bosque Farms, 1935. Dorothea Lange.
LC-USF 34-1639-E

Above: A teacher and students at the temporary school, hastily erected when rehabilitation clients poured in. Bosque Farms, 1936. Arthur Rothstein.
LC-USF 34-2974-E

The Resettlement Administration was simply a real estate developer who operated at an advantage and kept control of nearly every aspect of its clients' lives.

Today, one of these Resettlement Administration developments, Bosque Farms, is a thriving community twenty miles south of Albuquerque, lying just a few miles west of the interstate along the Rio Grande. Though one dairy farm still operates, land is too expensive for most farmers, selling for as much as $27,000 for a half-acre plot. Fast-food restaurants, branch banks, car washes, and other modern establishments choke both sides of the road where Ray Mitchell once

had his dairy farm. At eighty-five, he is the only homesteader still left who was moved down from the Mills area by the Resettlement Administration in the 1930s. He spends his days chain smoking and watching television with his second wife, Myrtle.

Like his fellow homesteaders, Mitchell originally came from someplace else (Oklahoma). He arrived in Harding County and thought it was the promised land. Like the others, the Mitchell experience followed the usual pattern. The land eventually turned to dust and they, too, went broke. For a few years Mitchell, trying to make ends meet, drove a school bus and sold cream to the creamery at Roy; he even tried to farm a little, but by 1932, he "couldn't stick a pick in the ground with the sharp end."

In April 1935, having forfeited everything he owned to the government, and with eighty dollars in his pocket from his last month's pay as a school bus driver, Mitchell departed for Bosque Farms with his wife and children. He had purchased an old school bus and tied a number of cages on top containing 100 laying hens. "You could tell where we went," he says, "by the trail of broken eggs that rolled down from the top onto the road."

Only three other Resettlement Administration clients were at Bosque Farms when he arrived. While the chickens went to roost in the cottonwood trees, Mitchell and his family moved into a government hay barn with three other families, each with its own space partitioned off from the others. Each family had agreed to clear the land of numerous cottonwood trees, some of them five feet in diameter, in order to make the land suitable for dairy farming. When the work was done, the Resettlement Administration agreed to sell the families fifty to ninety cleared acres of land for their dairy farms.

"It was terrible land," Ray Mitchell recalls. "Too many trees. You couldn't get the stumps out with the horses they brought in, so they bought tractors. After that, you had to level it out with a fresno. Took three years." Even then, he says, he did not like his land down by the river. "Full of sand and mosquitoes." Eventually he traded for a sixty-six-acre plot along the road, paying $140 an acre in 1940, a price nearly five times higher than for similar land nearby. But the government offered him a house with a red cement floor, running water, electricity, and a forty-year mortgage at 3 percent.

Ray Mitchell was a resourceful man. His family had never gone hungry, and he always managed to improve his condition. For the first five years, while he was waiting for the government to sell him his land, he sold eggs, then he helped break a herd of wild horses that the government sent in to assist with the land clearing work; after that, he was a WPA "progress foreman" earning a dollar an hour to oversee the clearing of trees and construction of the schoolhouse and dam. At one point he even shot and butchered 120 head of cattle confiscated from Dust Bowl refugees like himself. "I used a .22," he says with evident pride, "and it never took more than one shot to bring 'em down." The meat was offered to Bosque Farms residents at ten cents a pound, but most were too poor to afford the luxury of meat.

Once he had bought his land, Ray Mitchell became a dairy farmer on his sixty-six acres. While many Resettlement Administration clients got fed up with dairy farming and left, Ray Mitchell stayed on, eventually selling three different herds "for more money than I ever got for milk." Reaching a newfound prosperity, he paid off his land in ten years and burned his mortgage. In time, he sold most of his land, too, for $600 and more an acre. He believes that hard work and good fortune account for his success; he also says that if the government had not helped him, he "would have like to starve to death."

Today Ray Mitchell is a proud yet puzzled man. He resents the influx of "ousiders" who have driven the price of land sky high. According to his own count, 7,000 cars pass by his front door each day. "You just do what you gotta do," he says. "I was luckier than most, I reckon. You can make it if you don't give up. You gotta have some stick-to." Then, looking out the window toward the mess he thinks Bosque Farms has become, he says, "I don't think none of these fellers would survive the kind of life we knew."

Right: Workers make adobe bricks, turning them to dry in the sun. Bosque Farms, 1935. Dorothea Lange.
LC-USF 34-1648-E

CHAPTER TWO

PIE TOWN

It was the Great Depression and we had decided to get out of Texas. High dry winds blew from the West. Clouds of red dust filled the skies. Blue Northers came day after day. Cows lay dead everywhere. Banks foreclosed on farms and ranches. We lost almost all. My father, mother, me, and Jess, the family bull dog, left in a Model A, off to what promised to be a new life for all. . . . We arrived in Pie Town on July 4, 1933.

Edd Jones, homesteader, Pie Town

We came up here from Texas and thought we was in tall cotton. We didn't know we was poor till somebody told us. We didn't know we was working hard till somebody told us. It's how it always was. We didn't know anything else.

Maudie Belle McKee, homesteader's wife, Pie Town

There's a difference between being poor and being broke. When you're broke, you give up hope. When you're poor, you don't have money, that's all.

Bob Magee, homesteader, Pie Town

(Note: All photographs were taken by Russell Lee in June 1940.)

Opposite: Main street. Craig and Keele general store is the hub of Pie Town community life.
LC-USF 34-36796-D

We was poor as God's old dog and one-eyed as hell.

Rex Norris, homesteader, Pie Town

When Russell Lee arrived in Pie Town in June 1940, he found a thriving community that had been homesteaded by a group of twentieth-century pioneers only a few years before. Most of them were former Texas and Oklahoma sharecroppers, day laborers who had worked from sunup to sundown for a share of the profits from cotton, soybeans, corn, and other cash crops. Because of the drought, most of these sharecroppers eventually left, but some, like one man from Snyder, Texas, refused to give up hope. Every day he set off a charge of powder, trying to get clouds to form and rain to fall.

Like thousands of other Dust Bowl refugees, this particular group headed west, one and two families at a time, hoping to start over in the promised land. They did not end up in California but in Catron County, a land so vast that, as one homesteader put it, "the sky just run on forever" and "the wind felt like it come straight out of a shotgun barrel." Some families ended up in Pie Town simply because they ran out of money there, others because they had relatives nearby. Still others came because they'd heard about all the "free land" from someone down the road; they expected to get their share.

Pie Town was one of the last places in America still open for homesteading in the 1930s. Jefferson's original concept of "land for the landless" was supposed to turn ordinary Americans, many of them immigrants, into landholders, with the promise of 160 free acres apiece, later amended to 640 acres in the arid West. To get clear title, one had to "prove up," that is, to plant trees and to build a "permanent" dwelling, often nothing more than a heap of boards or logs. When the Homestead Act came to an end

Opposite: Pie Town homesteaders of the thirties filed on sections of Bill Dahl's huge W Bar ranch, carved out of public lands ten years earlier. Such action provoked violence against the homesteaders by big ranchers in the area who felt the land belonged to them.
LC-USF 34-36818-D

Right: Homesteader pumping water from a well owned by Harmon Craig. Few farmers can afford their own wells in this arid area where water is in short supply—and expensive.
LC-USF 33-12743-M5

in 1934, a provision was left for certain western lands to be claimed, but the acreage was reduced to 320 acres, barely enough, as one Pie Town homesteader put it, "to even piss on." The land that was left was submarginal, like that in Catron County, ignored by previous homesteaders because of its high altitude and poor soil.

This rugged countryside slopes away from the Continental Divide, a few miles east, and is covered with rabbit brush, sage, and piñon. At the time of Lee's arrival, some two hundred homesteader families were living in crude dugouts, tents, and small log cabins scattered along the dusty backroads. There was no doctor, dentist, or lawyer in Pie Town; there were no telephones, no running water or electricity. The nearest railroad was at Magdalena, sixty-five miles away; telegrams came from either Datil or Quemado, each about twenty miles distant. As Lee wrote in his notebook: "The main means of contact with the outside world is by the stage, which makes a round trip through Pie Town daily. The stage brings the mail, newspapers, express shipments, and sundry supplies in addition to any passengers who might be traveling through this remote region."

The scene he described in 1940 might have been anywhere in the nineteenth-century West. Indeed, as Lee soon discovered, Pie Town *was* a frontier town, complete with trail drives, Indians (mostly Navajos who came in the fall to pick piñon nuts), and a wealth of local lore. It was rumored that, a few miles north, a renegade named Gus Raney shot trespassers on sight, with his wife keeping watch from the top of the windmill; some said that Raney, in a fit of temper, had even drowned his own two sons in a stock tank. The post office at nearby Tres Lagunas had recently been robbed of three dollars: The robber had gotten as far as a mesa top where a posse found him taking a nap. A woman, known only as the Goat Girl, had been murdered out on the land where she kept her goats and "nested" (i.e., lived illegally on land claimed by someone else). Ghosts of Indians who lived in the area as long ago as 1500 B.C. were said to come back at night and cast spells. A family of eighteenth-century Spanish homesteaders who were murdered by Apaches came back, too, searching for their lost child, abducted by the Indians. So the stories went.

Undaunted by the tales he heard from townspeople, Lee and his wife, Jean, decided to stay in the tiny, log Pie Town Hotel and rented all of its three rooms, one of which had a view of two

privies, a well, and a chicken coop. Lee liked what he saw in Pie Town, and he wanted to make a complete record of it. He set out in his 1938 Chevrolet, "armed with a crude map" and all his cameras. It did not take him long to find out about his surroundings and the people who lived there.

Following World War I, homesteaders trickled into the Pueblo Plateau. They were almost all from Texas, and most meant to raise stock on their 640 acres. Clyde Norman, an ex-service man, came to Catron County at the close of the world war, lured by the promise of free land. He soon tangled with local ranchers, squatters on what was then government land, who outnumbered Mr. Norman by a hundred to one. Refusing to be driven out, Clyde Norman filed a

Above: Entrance to the three-room Pie Town Hotel where Russell and Jean Lee spent three weeks in 1940, using one room as a darkroom.
LC-USF 34-36875-D

Right: The daily stage from Socorro brings in mail, freight, express, and passengers. Boxes tied to the fender contain live chicks.
LC-USF 34-36739-D

mining claim on forty acres at the present location of Pie Town and called it "Norman's Place" (so designated on old state highway maps). He went into the oil, gas, and grocery business first and later opened a small eating place where he served coffee and food in a one-room picket house. But Mr. Norman, a bachelor who only learned to cook what he called "essentials"—beans, grits, and chicken fried steak—discovered that cowboys wanted dessert. He bought doughnuts from the bakery at Datil, twenty miles away, traveling back and forth over the dirt roads in a Model T Ford. His trade grew until the little bakery could not supply his demand for doughnuts. A rancher's wife who had financed the Datil bakery suggested that he "build pies" at his place and name the village Pie Town. A kindly neighbor is said to have assisted Mr. Norman in his first baking attempts.

Pie Town slumbered along for a dozen years until 1932 when Harmon L. Craig, a Spanish-American War veteran who had lost most of his money during the bank failure at Magdalena, bought a half-interest in Pie Town. Reportedly, he paid $200 and a cow for his share. Mr. Craig started adding other baked products to Mr. Norman's limited menu, as well as a few mercantile items. Eventually he bought out Mr. Norman's half-interest and the latter returned to Texas. Mr. Craig, now the sole owner of the town, married Theodora Baugh, a Texas divorcee with two daughters. The three women, baking night and day, turned out pies, cakes, and cookies said to have been famous for a hundred miles. Cowboys on the long cattle drives always took time out to stop for pie and coffee. Pie Town became legendary as having the best pies in the state.

While the women baked, Craig expanded his business, put in gas pumps, groceries, tires, and tack, and eventually had his store declared an official U.S. post office; it was also an official "stage stop" where such items as live chicks came on a weekly run from Santa Fe. But it was during the depression, when sharecroppers were trying to make a go of their homesteads, that H. L. Craig helped out. He would lend money to the struggling farmers, at no interest, and with no collateral other than their word. Mr. Craig also showed homesteaders how to make harnesses out of old tires and sold them land at less than market value. He provided a house that served as the school where Grace Lucas taught; her salary came out of the homesteaders' own pockets for three years.

After hearing these reports, Russell Lee went to see Harmon L. Craig, who by then was in partnership with a man named Keele. Mr. Craig's establishment was at the core of the town's existence, and he was the man behind it. Lee found him to be "a short man with long arms, and the kind of voice I associated with people who had lived a happy life."

In a *U.S. Camera* article (October 1941), Lee quoted Craig,

> Yes, most of the people arrived in Pie Town without any money. Usually they brought their kids, their personal belongings, some articles of furniture, some family heirlooms. They came in cars which barely made the grade. Once they arrived, our people helped them to locate the land to be homesteaded. They'd get together

Opposite: Harmon Craig sits on sacks of homegrown pinto beans before hauling them to market. Mr. Craig allows local farmers to store surplus beans in his warehouse free of charge during the winter months. He also makes them interest-free loans.
LC-USF 34-36774-D

Above: Roberta Emery, left, fixes the hair of her neighbor, Etta Mae McKee, in a corner of the grocery store. Since there is no beauty shop for eighty miles, all the women take turns fixing each others' hair.
LC-USF 34-36748-D

Right: Mrs. Holley dishes up ice cream in the cafe owned by her daughter and son-in-law.
LC-USF 34-36688-D

and build them a dugout; give them some canned goods if they needed them.

In the early days we made our own farming tools. We've made our own plows; constructed harrows by driving spikes through piñon poles tied together. We used burros for a lot of power. In fact Leatherman over there does all his work with them now. At the store we've helped with credit. Now and then there's some work around here where a man can get some money for wages. . . .

At bean havest time most bean farmers bring their beans to the warehouse; I charge twenty-five cents a hundred [pounds] to clean them, furnish the sack and storage. We truck them to Socorro or Albuquerque and don't charge a cent. . . .

Harmon Craig, a modest man by Lee's account, went on to tell how the community had joined together on several projects, leaving out the fact that it was he who put up the money for materials.

We built the Farm Bureau together. We have a meeting the first Saturday of every month. Social life? Well, we built that church down the street a year ago—all of us got together on that, too. Every three months or so we have a community sing—people from all around come here to get together to sing. . . . Then we go over to their places to sing. We have our square dances, our literary society meetings, our 42 parties (that's a kind of dominoes they play in Texas), play parties, pie suppers, everything they used to do back home. Do they want to stay here? . . . For the first time in their lives these people own their land, and they feel they've got a future here. Sure, it's hard going, but a man can make it if he's willing to work.

Harmon Craig's homespun philosophy, and his analysis of the town, struck a responsive chord in Russell Lee, who had been reared in the Midwest. As he said later in an interview, "My objective required that I show what the people of Pie Town—the old, the young, the diligent, the frivolous, and the careworn—were like; wherein they were just folks and wherein each was a unique individual." He also wondered, as he wrote in *U.S. Camera,*

What was the relationship between the farmer and the business men? What were the lives of these people like? How did they get along without much money? What kind of farm tools did they have? And their clothes? their food? their health?

Did they have much social life—if so, was it the church, the Farm Bureau, or what? How did they feel about this country? Did they want

Above: Although homesteading offers little time for relaxation, an all-day community sing, held in the Baptist church, is the highlight of Pie Town social life.
LC-USF 33-12784-M5

Left: Left to right; Fred Hamilton, Lawrence Brown, Oscar Nicholson, and Jack Whinery join in the fun of a community sing.
LC-USF 34-36930-D

Above: Mrs. Bill Stagg, a homesteader's wife, putting the coffee on the table for dinner, which consists of home-cured ham and gravy, pinto beans, corn, homemade pickles, homegrown tomatoes, homemade bread and hot biscuits, fruit salad, cake, two kinds of pie, milk, and coffee.
LC-USF 34-36660-D

Right: Jack Whinery building a fence on his homestead.
LC-USF 34-36710-D

to go back to Texas or Oklahoma? Or did they want to make this their home?

Lee had been trained in this kind of thorough documentary approach by Roy Stryker and by his own observations after nearly four years in the field as an FSA photographer. He wondered about details, relationships between people and land, and the dynamics of change, as well as the historical roots of people, places, and things.

He began photographing the town and the land around it, the local cafe, garage, and Craig's mercantile. He was fascinated by this store where "a pail of drinking water was hung up shoulder-high where anyone could quench his thirst" and by the fact that the store was also where local women could get their hair done. The garage caught his interest as a place where "tires were inflated and changed, burros watered, wagons repaired by the farmers themselves."

Soon after he arrived, Russell Lee met a thirty-year-old homesteader from Oklahoma named Faro Caudill, his wife, Doris, and their five-year-old daughter, Josie. Caudill's strong good looks, his dugout home, laboriously constructed from logs hauled down from the mountains, and his deter-

mination to make a go of pinto bean farming, impressed Lee. He quoted him in *U.S. Camera*,

The advertisements used to say nature in the raw is seldom mild and they must have been talking about homesteading, because it isn't an easy life we've got here—our growing season's short. I've got to get my seed in the ground the day we're clear of frost (which is usually the last day of May) or else when the frosts come again in October my beans won't be matured for the harvest. . . . We came without money, we've had to grub and clear our own land, dig our wells, build our corrals and barns as well as our houses. But we don't go hungry, that's one thing. We raise our own meat and this land sure grows garden stuff. Doris cans enough to last the winter through. Not that she's doing anything extra, all the women do.

Russell Lee's greatest pleasure came from a night spent at a square dance held at Bill Stagg's log cabin. As he later wrote in *U.S. Camera*,

In one corner the orchestra, consisting of fiddle and two guitars, was tuning up. Square dances, Paul Jones, broom dances, round dances, individual exhibitions by the women and men followed in rapid succession. The children slept in the other wing of the house.

At midnight there was intermission for food,

Above: Former Texas sharecropper Oley "Monk" McKee dances a jig at Bill Stagg's all-night party.
LC-USF 34-36912-D

Left: Babysitters are unheard of in Pie Town, so parents bring their children to a party and put them to bed. LC-USF 34-36884-D

Right: Etta Mae McKee, left, dances with an unidentified partner at Bill Stagg's party.
LC-USF 34-36870-D

cakes, cookies, pies, coffee. Somebody produced two cases of beer—it was rapidly consumed. The party went back to the dance. Bill Stagg forgot his game leg, Adams forgot that he hadn't danced for three years, Les Thomas let himself go. The orchestra played with more pep and zip. The jigging started—it became an informal contest. They were still whooping it up at 4 a.m. when I had to go back to town to change film.

Pie Town is not much of a town anymore, just a wide spot on U.S. 60 where it crosses the Continental Divide at an elevation of 8,000 feet, with a few modest frame houses on either side of the road. As towns go, it lacks most amenities: there is no school, bank, hotel, barber shop, drugstore, movie theater, restaurant, gas station, newspaper stand, super market, doctor, lawyer, dentist, or law enforcement officer. There is still a cafe (that serves, predictably, a wide assortment of homemade pies) with a small grocery in back, a post office, two churches, a cemetery, a fire station, and a curio shop that is open one or two days a week during the summer tourist season. Everything else is boarded up or falling down, including most of the buildings photographed by Russell Lee. Pie Town seems ready to pass into oblivion.

Harmon Craig's mercantile, the gas station

where Mr. Leatherman drove his mule wagon to get the tires changed, the old post office where the stage came through once a day, the three-room Pie Town Hotel, Lois Stagg's cafe, have all been closed or torn down. In addition to the Baptist church where Lee photographed the congregation one Sunday morning, there is now a Mormon church, shunned by old-timers who still prefer the Baptist church. The schoolhouse is now a summer home owned by a Texas family who call it "Journey's End." The community center still stands, though there are no more Farm Bureau meetings, literary society debates, or all-day community sings. Occasionally, a country band comes from Socorro or Quemado and plays until morning. Even schoolchildren attend, swinging small partners until their parents take them home. There is a new fire station, but the former male fire chief has been replaced by a woman who won in a narrow election forced by Pie Town women tired of the old regime. The streets where Russell Lee pointed his lens are rutted, many of the slab-side houses with wells and privies in the back are boarded up; in the backyards, a rusted wheelbarrow, a high-laced shoe, a dishpan used for target practice, a home-made swing, and a lady's bonnet are all that remain of a bygone era.

Left: Mr. Leatherman drives his burro-drawn cart up to the filling station to get air in the rubber tires. He is a pinto bean farmer, and the local Baptist preacher.
LC-USF 33-12726-M5

Above right: The Pie Town cafe, said to have the best pies in New Mexico, attracts cowboys and farmers from all of Catron County.
LC-USF 34-36773-D

The townspeople—the hundred or so that are left—are mostly older people who have lived there a long time. A few, like the Roy McKees, Rex Norris, and George Hutton, still remember Russell Lee and the time he spent there. Many have his Pie Town pictures framed on the wall or pasted into scrapbooks. These families, like everyone else there, have large gardens that may be struck with a hard frost in June, television sets that connect them to an unfamiliar world, and pickup trucks that they use to haul everything from sick cattle to parts for their backyard wells. Townspeople think nothing of driving eighty miles to Socorro for groceries or a medical appointment. Isolated, stubborn, and forged by the elements around them, the people of Pie Town have learned to make do with the means at hand.

"After the Dust Bowl, it looked like heaven to us," recalls Maudie Belle McKee, who arrived in Pie Town with her husband, Roy, and their two small children in 1936.

We had to leave that blowed-out country [West Texas]. It was so bad when the northers come. The stillness would be so still. The darkness was like night in the middle of the day. The dust come in every crack and you'd leave it for two or three days till the wind wore itself out. I remember one day we was havin' my folks down to dinner and I made a coconut cream pie with meringue on top. Time we got ready to eat, one of them dust storms hit. The meringue was the same color as the beans.

The daughter of a Texas rice and cotton share-cropper, Maudie Belle was one of eight children who lived in a two-room shack most of her childhood. She learned to make do. "You just planned your days around the troubles and worries that you had," she says with the sort of frontier philosophy that characterizes so many women of her generation. "We didn't know any different. We had stock, we had lots of hogs, we had milk cows. My mother had turkeys she raised and sold in the fall. Hard times? We didn't know any different. It was all we ever knew. Yes,

Left: Mrs. Bill Stagg with a state quilt she made while she "rested" during the noon hour. Mrs. Stagg helps her husband in the fields with plowing, planting, weeding corn, and harvesting beans.
LC-USF 34-36692-D

Below: Nothing goes to waste in Pie Town. Mrs. Whinery makes a fly swatter from a scraps of screen, oilcloth, and a coat hanger.
LC-USF 34-36604-D

Right: Mrs. Whinery's dugout kitchen has a dirt floor and simple furnishings, no water or electricity, but here she cans, bakes, and cooks for her family.
LC-USF 33-12739-M5

they was hard times. They was all the times there was."

"That old dust kinda put us out of business," says Roy McKee who made, in a good year like 1935, about $200 sharecropping cotton.

> It was enough to live on though because we growed all our own food. Mama made all our own clothes or patched up the old ones and kept us a-goin'. We had lots of chickens and raised hogs. Only you couldn't sell 'em. Sometimes I'd take a team of mules and a big old cotton wagon and go fifteen, twenty miles and haul them old melons that grows wild over in the sand hills.

Once his hogs were fattened on melons, McKee gave them to his neighbors. But finally, in 1936, the drought, the dust, and the depression became too much for Roy McKee. He drove a 1928 John Deere tractor, "with a trailer load of junk," 400 miles from his home in West Texas all the way to Pie Town. Because the tractor had no lights, McKee could only drive during the daylight hours. The trip took ten days. "It wasn't easy," he says of driving along U.S. 60 to Pie Town. "It was just a couple of ruts, like a wagon road. Everywhere you looked, there was somebody broke down. Okies. Dusted out like us."

The place was high, wild, and desolate. But to these refugees, this immense windswept land bounded by low mountains and mesas on all sides offered a respectable way to start over. They arrived in Pie Town by the dozens, and unpacked their trucks and wagons, stacked high with beds, stoves, furniture, utensils, even chickens and pigs. One family survived the long haul by eating eggs that the chickens laid in a cage at the back of their truck, and slaughtered the pig when they got there. They shot deer out of season and ate jack rabbits, squirrels, and vegetables from their gardens. Like most homesteaders, they believed that all they had to do was work hard, stay together, and with God's help, manage to survive.

Above: The first step for newly arrived homesteaders is to clear the land of sagebrush. Fred Caudill witches for water after his son, Faro, has cleared the land. A forked stick twitches and is mysteriously yanked downward over the proper location for a well.
LC-USF 33-12750-M2

Below: Jack Whinery, using a homemade plow and mules, prepares his field for planting pinto beans.
LC-USF 33-12746-M4

Right: The Housell brothers, using a model T Ford, plow a field they've recently cleared of sagebrush and cedars.
LC-USF 34-36568-D

"We got to Pie Town with four dollars in our pockets," recalls another homesteader, sixty-nine-year-old Rex Norris, who arrived in 1935 from Texas with his father and two brothers. The family arrived in a Model T truck, "a yodelin' Tom," into which they'd piled all their belongings. The four Norris men went to work at the local sawmill, receiving a dollar each for a ten-hour day, and "there wasn't no overtime either." Norris still lives on his original homestead, raising chickens, a few cattle, including a milk cow, hogs, pinto beans, and corn. His seventy-three-year-old bachelor brother, Granville, known affectionately as "Granny," lives on an adjoining homestead; he spends most of his time planning the annual Norris family reunion, held each August, which attracts as many as three hundred family members from all over the country.

Rex Norris's life is simple and rewarding, steeped in long experience with the earth and seasons. His thirty-seven-year-old second wife, Patty, shares it with him, living much as other pioneer women who came half a century earlier. She cans vegetables from the garden, bakes bread, makes butter, washes clothing with a primitive washing machine, and cooks on an old wood stove. In her spare time she works in her mother's cafe in Pie Town, quilts with the other women, and serves as a volunteer firewoman. Their three sons, ranging in age from twelve to three, help with the chores, chopping wood, feeding the animals, and working in the garden. The boys love animals, especially a recent litter of puppies, their milk cow, and their horses. On Sundays, the family attends the First Baptist Church, which Rex helped to build in 1939.

"I wouldn't say it was easy," says Norris about his homesteading days. "It was the only life we knew." He adds, "We done it all ourselves. They can look in the records and see. We never drawed one penny of relief." Now, in his later years, Rex Norris is proud of the fact that he owns his place free and clear and doesn't "owe one thin dime to nobody, but I could borrow if I wanted to."

Through back-breaking work from sunup to sun-down, the Norrises and other families eventually "proved up" on their homestead, grubbing out hundreds of acres of thick-rooted piñon and sage by hand in order to plant pinto beans. Sometimes it took a month just to clear one acre. Until this time, no cash crops had ever been grown successfully on the Pueblo Plateau. So great was the determination of these home-steaders, however, that one farmer was able to harvest a small tobacco crop for which he won first prize at the Catron County Fair.

Not one man actually made a living planting pinto beans, although dozens tried. All were forced to take jobs elsewhere in order to survive. Some farmers worked for the WPA, others at Harmon Craig's mercantile, or at the local saw-mill; still others were employed by the WPA as road graders, ditch diggers, and surveyors. They earned $1.50 a day, but no one complained for they were able to make ends meet. After a stint at the sawmill, Rex Norris worked as a trapper for the New Mexico Fish and Game Department, a job he held for thirty-five years. During this time he also became an amateur archaeologist, uncovering prehistoric Indian sites in the remote areas where he went to trap coyotes and moun-tain lions.

Roy McKee was a well driller for forty-three years, bringing precious water to most of his neighbors' homes. "I didn't make no real money at it," he says. "I just believed in heppin' peo-ple." In addition to her duties as frontier wife and the mother of six children, Maudie Belle served as the Pie Town postmistress for twenty-two years. "They never did get used to it," she says of her family, especially Roy, who felt that Maudie Belle's working meant that his efforts to provide for his family had never been sufficient.

Today, the resourceful Roy McKee, retired from the well-drilling business, is the undisputed piñon nut king of Pie Town; he and his workers painstakingly gather about 5,000 pounds a sea-son. Once, a record crop of 40,000 pounds, stored in his nephew's living room, went straight through the floor. McKee and his workers use the old method of shaking the piñon trees, but the biggest hauls come from raids on ground-level rats' nests, which often yield as much as a hundred pounds of nuts each. "The ol' rat, he jes' piles it in agin," he says, "and we come along and dig it out agin. The ol' rat don't never catch on."

Few of these homesteaders care to admit that Pie Town, along with much of the homesteaded West, was not the agrarian utopia they had dreamed of; here it took as many as 100 acres just to keep one cow and calf alive. But the set-tlement satisfied people's craving for roots and continuity, themes that had implanted them-selves deeply in the imagination of nineteenth-century America and continued well into the twentieth century. Pie Town was living proof of an enduring belief that one had only to work hard, raise a family, and master nature in order to attain freedom and betterment. In the words of noted historian Henry Nash Smith, "The char-acter of the American empire was defined not by streams of influence out of the past, not by a cultural tradition, nor by its place in a world community, but by a relation between man and nature—or rather, even more narrowly, between American man and the American West."

In Pie Town, people and the American West were quickly joined. One of the earliest home-steaders, George Hutton, lived a few miles northwest of Pie Town on a piñon-studded ridge. "We were the first," he said with characteristic pride, "except for ol' Bob Magee over there to Adams' Diggins. Him and his family come in 1917, before the rest of us. They were from Kan-sas though," he said, as if that made a difference. The Huttons came from Oklahoma in 1931 and filed a claim on 640 acres. They began clearing the land where the hand-hewn log cabin still stands. "Mama refused to live in a tent," he said. "Or a dugout either. She wanted a log cabin, so me and dad had to build her one even before we got the pinto beans in."

Hutton made his home in this same log cabin for fifty-six years, until his death in 1987. Dur-ing the last few years, his daughter-in-law, Rose, a solid chain-smoking woman and her thirty-four-year-old daughter, Pat, who has never mar-ried, lived with him. His only son, Ollie, died in 1986, a tragedy from which he never really recovered. Both of George's wives had left him years ago. "They couldn't stand this kind of life," he said one day as he showed a visitor around the cluttered log home where Rose and her daughter were making a quilt on a frame hanging from the living room ceiling. Russell Lee had photographed this same room in 1940; nothing much had changed, not even the furni-ture or the pictures on the wall.

A large, overweight man in bib overalls, Hutton moved slowly that day because the arthritis in his legs was bothering him. He com-plained that he could no longer plant pinto beans or drive a tractor or ride a horse. "All us old-

Opposite above: Mrs. George Hutton, Sr., refused to live in a tent or a dugout after her arrival from Oklahoma in 1931. Her husband and son built a log cabin for her, and dug a well.
LC-USF 34-36678-D

Below: Mrs. Hutton prepares to do the family laundry in an improvised washing machine built by her son, George, Jr.
LC-USF 33-12727-M1

timers are wore out," he said. "Can't hardly do a day's work anymore." For a once-active man like Hutton, such a situation was hard to bear.

For years, Hutton had gone out to work while his father stayed home and farmed. "We had one good year, '39, when pintos got up to nineteen cents a pound. Reckon we made a couple thousand dollars that year. We thought we was rich," he said. Hutton eventually added another 640-acre section to his family's original claim, making him one of the largest landowners around. In order to add to his stake, he held jobs as a welder, plumber, blacksmith, logger, steelworker, electrician, cowboy, and machinist, sometimes taking jobs as far away as California. He was often away for months at a time. "I done everything it was honorable to do," he said, "just to keep this old place alive." Hutton was proud of the fact that no one in Pie Town ever applied for New Deal relief, preferring to, as he put it, "prove up on ourselves. The only handout we wanted was the government's hand out of our pockets."

He led his visitor through the woodworking shop where he was making an inlaid coffee table. He was also an accomplished leather worker who made his own saddles, chaps, and gun cases. When he was finished with the tour, George Hutton sat down on an old chair outside. "Some say it's just old scrub country, but to me its kinda pretty," he said, looking out over a back-yard cluttered with old automobile and truck chassis, rusted machinery, wash tubs, and other artifacts of his tenure there. "I wouldn't live no place else but here."

George Hutton and his fellow homesteaders, like their nineteenth-century counterparts, were faced with constant hardships. Drought wiped them out several years in a row; early snowstorms froze crops before harvest; summer brought grasshoppers and mealy worms. Banks would not lend them money so they developed an iron-hard will common to the frontier. Local ranchers called them "nesters," "squatters," and worse. Violence erupted for years. One homesteader discovered his dog shot in the backyard. Another had all his fences ripped down. A year's supply of hay mysteriously caught fire. In town, the "Okies" had their tires slashed while they were inside buying supplies. Thugs hired by ranchers came and tried to beat them up, even posing as government agents in an effort to drive the homesteaders out. When one such imposter showed up, George Hutton told him, "I reckon there's enough land out here for me and you both."

Roy McKee, who stands at six and a half feet tall in his bare feet, encountered one thug toting a .45 and threw him off his land. He recalls, "I jus' reached up inside his shirt and said, 'You're yaller. You ain't gonna pull that gun,' and sort of rubbed my fist in his face. Reckon I made a believer out of him." As Rex Norris tells it, "We come through lots worse than some ol' crazy boy tryin' to run us off." Then he adds, "Ol' Roy was an inspiration to us all. He'd even fight a circle saw."

The people who are left say they will stay there forever, that nothing can drive them away, even if the whole town falls down. Rex Norris hopes that one of his three boys will want his place someday; Granville Norris plans to leave

his homestead to Rex's boys; Roy McKee says that he hopes his kids will want to use his homestead as a summer home. George Hutton left his place to his grandchildren. All of these homesteaders, like their fathers before them, want to be buried in the Pie Town cemetery so that, as Granny Norris once said, "We can be close to our neighbors." Every Memorial Day, the people of Pie Town gather with relatives from all around and clean the place up. "It's kinda nice," says Rex Norris, "knowin' somebody cares."

Edd Jones was the man behind the pies of Pie Town for more than twenty years, from 1933 until Harmon Craig's former cafe closed down in 1954. Now eighty-three years old, Edd Jones is a tiny spectre of a man who lives alone in a primitive cabin "up there on Allegre," the 11,000-foot-high landmark south of town. He and his parents came to Pie Town in 1933, Dust Bowl refugees from Fluanna, Texas, where he started keeping a journal of those difficult years. ("I always wanted to be a writer," he says, "ever since I got out of Texas A and M.") Mr. and Mrs. Jones had enough money left from the sale of what was left of the family ranch in Texas to buy 640 acres on the heavily wooded Allegre, a part of Catron County not open to homesteading.

They tried to ranch, but the high altitude ruined their operation. "Snows seven months out of the year up there," Edd Jones says. He claims he was luckier than most because he got a job in Lois Stagg's cafe the first month he got here; she had bought the place the year before from Harmon Craig's wife. Jones was able to help support his family through his work at the cafe until both his parents died. "It's why I never married," he says. "I had my mother and father to take care of." Now, in his old age, there is no one to take care of him except for neighbors like the Norrises and the McKees who look in on him once in a while. Rex Norris has a copy of Edd Jones's will, including directions about his burial under a favorite ponderosa tree.

"I reckon I made forty, fifty thousand pies before I was through," Edd Jones says. He worked for a dollar a day for a number of years, but "all my meals was free." He says he made seventy-five pies a week, year in and year out, which comes close to 78,000 pies during the twenty years he worked for Mrs. Stagg. He says he remembers when Russell Lee was there taking pictures of the Stagg family, but he hid in the pantry to avoid having his picture taken. "I ain't so photogenic," he says.

Edd Jones considers himself a master pie

baker, "as good as any man alive." He does not share his secrets with everyone, he says, but he tells his visitor some things to remember about making good pies: A quarter-cup of water for two pie crusts, more than that will make them tough as shoe leather. A handful of lard, not oleo or butter. Don't boil the milk, it will take the sweetness out. Let the pie cool naturally. "Worst thing in the world is to put a pie in the refrigerator. Even setting it on the windowsill ain't good."

Walking stiffly with a cane, Edd Jones takes his visitor on a tour of Pie Town, accompanied by his thirteen-year-old terrier, Midge. He uses the cane as a pointer to show the places where his memories are stored. The post office is now a sagging shed. Arch McPaul was the postmaster, "a good ol' boy." Over there was where J. V. Wyche had his taxidermy shop. "Sometimes you could go in and see a dozen deer heads all lined up. Elk and bobcat and grizzly bear. Ol' J. V. liked to fix their mouths in a smile so folks'd think they died happy."

"Here's where Aubrey Redwine had his garage. Fixed flats for a dime. Over there was Guy

Melton's barber shop. Haircuts cost a quarter. Lois's cafe was right there among them weeds, behind the Eagle Gas store. We never did have no menu. There was only one entree, but lots and lots of pies. Apple. Cherry. Custard. At Christmas, mince and pumpkin."

He says he remembers when Pie Town got electricity (1942) and telephone service (1962). He never had plumbing, so he doesn't remember when water got hooked up. People left, he says, because the war came along and they got jobs in factories, building ships and bombs. Faro Caudill went to Alaska and never did come back to Pie Town. "Give his homestead away," he says. "It's how a lotta guys got rich, buyin' up homesteads real cheap, dollar an acre, even less." The people left in Pie Town are "the real people. They ain't nuthin' gonna drive 'em out. Not an earthquake, not the gov'mint."

Edd Jones wears his customary baseball cap with "SUNBUM" emblazoned across the crown, a pair of baggy trousers two sizes too big, a cowboy shirt with pearl snap buttons. His shoes are the same ones he's had for thirty years; he never throws anything away until it wears out. He

Left: On a lonely rural road several miles from their homestead, the Huttons and their neighbors receive mail.
LC-USF 34-35863-D

Right: A farmer hauling water home through the sagebrush. Sometimes a homesteader does not have the equipment or money to dig his own well, so he must haul water for household and stock.
LC-USF 34-36812-D

looks as if he hasn't shaved in several weeks, yet a grizzled look becomes him. He raises his cane and points. Across the street was Frank Wilson's bar, ten cents a drink. Edd says he ought to know. But the doc doesn't want him to drink anymore. Bad for his heart. He moves on to the Craig and Keele mercantile; here is the core of what he likes to remember best. The town's foremost citizen is still a hero in the old man's mind.

"Mr. Craig was a red-headed cowboy from Washington state who first worked for W. C. Dahl on his ranch south of town," he says with pride at being Pie Town's main historian. "He owned 160 acres right here where we're at, sold it to build the town. He had two little jackasses that he farmed twenty acres with, plowed and planted with 'em till they got wore out. Everything gets wore out. Even Mr. Craig. He worked hisself to death. He's over yonder in the cemetery. Every once in a while I go over there and I say, 'Mr. Craig, do you ever wonder how it all turned out?'"

CHAPTER THREE

HISPANIC VILLAGES

My ancestors came to this valley way back, with the conquistadores. They had land, but over the years they lost it. Now we have only this little bit left, but it's enough to get by on.

Carmen Velarde, Ranchos de Taos

I was born poor and raised poor and what's the difference if I die and they dig a trench and put me in it? If you want to give me flowers, do it now so I can smell them while I'm still alive.

Ofelia Lopez, Las Trampas

Everything I have I owe to my dad and mom. They taught us to work hard and save our money. I own 100 acres and 80 head of purebred sheep. I don't owe a peso to anybody. I am a happy man.

Blas Chávez, Los Cordovas

I'd rather die today than sin tomorrow.

Tony Chávez, Taos

Tener bastante con nada, que nosotros. (*To have enough with nothing, that's us.*)

Antonio Romero, Rodarte

Opposite: A widow sits beneath portraits of her family. Peñasco, 1943. John Collier, Jr.
LC-USW 3-13688-C

In December 1942, John Collier, Jr., was sent to New Mexico by Roy Stryker to photograph 700-year-old Taos Pueblo in northern New Mexico. It was the dead of winter, and the Indians were in their "quiet time," when all activity ceases and the Taos go into spiritual retreat. By this time, pictures of American rural life were all but completed; the efforts of the FSA, now under the auspices of the Office of War Information (OWI), were directed at the defense industry and the harmonious efforts of a united people. Collier had been at OWI a year and a half; during that time he had made stunning pictures of shipbuilders, Pennsylvania coal miners, Portuguese fishermen, and the Amish people of Lancaster (Pa.) County. He was ready for some-

thing different. Stryker called him into his office and offered him a trip back to his beloved New Mexico, where he had spent much of his childhood. His assignment: to document what Stryker called "the oldest democracy in America," an example of a way to counteract the global communist threat. That Taos Pueblo was anything but a democracy did not faze Collier.

In a 1987 interview, Collier said, "OWI thought they had a hot piece of democratic propaganda. I knew it wouldn't work, but I wanted to get out of the East." Because of his long association with the tribe, Collier knew that Taos Pueblo was a theocracy where religious elders decided issues on the basis of time-held beliefs. Nonetheless, he went before the tribal council

Opposite: Juan Lopez and his son haul wood out of the mountains near Las Trampas, 1943. John Collier, Jr.
LC-USW 3-15224-C

Right: Post office. Amalia, 1940. Russell Lee.
LC-USF 34-37065-D

and presented his case. They thought about it for days. Then they called him in. Recalls Collier,

They said, "We think you have a wonderful idea. You can take as many pictures as you want—of Jerry Mirabal." He was a postcard Indian who hung around the plaza. Everyone took pictures of him. I said thank you and went home.

I had to get justification to stay in New Mexico, so I made a connection with the medical clinic in Questa. It started as a New Deal project, and it was still going strong. I found that this was the first time the Hispanic people [of northern New Mexico] had had adequate medical care, so I photographed everything—people driving to the clinic in a horse-drawn buggy, waiting in the waiting room, being examined by the doctor. I photographed the dentist too, pulling out some child's tooth with a pair of pliers.

Then I found Father Smith, the parish priest. He used to translate the world news every night through his loudspeaker (mounted on top of his car). At this time [1943], Questa had the most despicable reputation of any town in New Mexico. No one cooperated with anyone else. So Father Smith decided to do something. One day he got an axe and started tearing down the

bridge, the only way in or out of town. When people saw what he was doing, they were furious. They said, "What are you doing that for?" And Father Smith said, "If I don't tear down the bridge, it'll fall down." The people said, "In that case, we'll help you." So they tore it down and then they realized what they had done. "Now we can't get out of town," they said. Father Smith said, "I guess you'll have to build another one." And they did.

Although the tale may have been apocryphal, Collier had a great time telling it. He went on.

Father Smith lived in a house on top of the hill. From there he could see everything that was going on in town—who was fighting, who was hanging out in the bars, and so forth. One day he had a police siren mounted on top of his car. Whenever he saw a disturbance, he'd turn on the siren and go down. He'd say to them, "Did you see it? Did you hear it? Then swallow it." He succeeded in remodeling Questa. Two years later, it won a prize for civil cooperation.

After my luck with Father Smith, I went over to Peñasco and attached myself to Father Cassidy. He was just a young priest then, not more than twenty-five years old, and very bright. I spent every evening having a religious

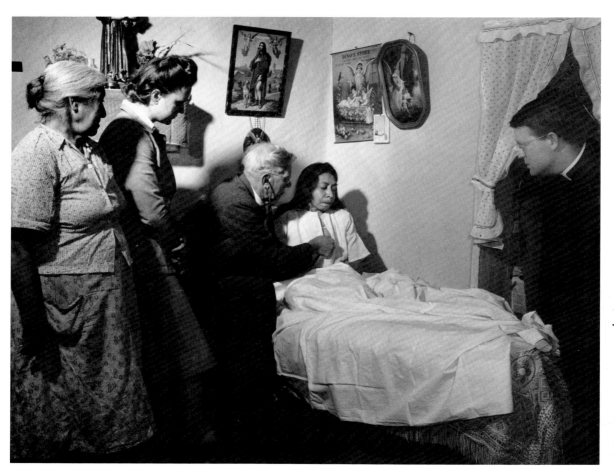

Left: Dr. Onstine of the Taos County Cooperative Health Association and Father Pat Smith at the bedside of a tubercular patient. Questa, 1943. John Collier, Jr.
LC-USW 3-17918-C

Right: Father Walter Cassidy saying mass in the eighteenth-century San José de Gracia Church. Las Trampas, 1943. John Collier, Jr.
LC-USW 3-14751-C

discussion with him in the rectory. I saw an opportunity to make an investigation into the Catholic faith, so I'd present Father Cassidy with a socio-drama to test the moral fiber of Catholicism.

He told me that there were eight moral circumstances where a person could actually kill someone and not be guilty for it, such as finding a man raping your mother or killing your children. You were supposed to use compassion, love, reason, and moral persuasion on him. Then, when you used up all the strategies, you were allowed to kill such a man, he said. The church would not find you guilty of mortal sin and consign you to hell. So I went to work and I got Father Cassidy to use up the eight circumstances. I don't remember what they were, but I structured them in such a way that they were the worst conditions I could think of. After I drove Father Cassidy to murder, he said, "I'm only talking to you to strengthen myself, John." He told me that you're judged at the gates of heaven for your conscience and since I had none, they couldn't keep me out.

Following this unusual encounter with Father Cassidy, Collier was introduced to the people of Las Trampas by the priest. ("They were pure flame," Collier said in the 1987 interview. "I shared myself with them.")

Although Father Cassidy does not recall the "socio-drama" outlined by John Collier, he does remember what Las Trampas was like when he arrived in 1939 to become their priest. "They were good, honest, hard-working people living there," he says, seated in the rectory of the parish in Albuquerque where he has spent the last seven years administering to the people of the barrio. "They reminded me of the people in Mora where I grew up. I felt at home in Las Trampas, in the whole Peñasco area actually. John and I went around and saw a number of families and he photographed them. His Spanish was none too good, so I'd interpret for him and he'd take pictures. We got along fine."

Now seventy-one years old, with a hint of Irish mischief in his eyes, Father Cassidy still has the strong, sensuous good looks of his youth. He grew up in Cleveland, a small town near Mora, the son of an Irish storekeeper and flour mill owner and a German mother who died when he was eight years old. As a boy he was a hell-raiser, fond of girls, dancing, and drinking. But he worked hard, too, in the mill and in the fields, helping to support his motherless family. He was also the manager of the local baseball

Above: Christmas eve in the church. Ranchos de Taos, 1942. John Collier, Jr. LC-USW 3-38417-C

Right: Father Cassidy is a priest involved in every aspect of his parishioners' lives. On his day off, he helps to appraise the value of the farm and equipment of a parishioner who wants to borrow money to purchase the farm. 1943. John Collier, Jr. LC-USW 3-17330-C

team, which was always in debt. Once, to raise money, he became a moonshiner, turning out fifty gallons of whiskey, which he sold for a dollar a quart. He bottled the brew in beer bottles and blue milk-of-magnesia bottles borrowed from his father's old store. At eighteen, he won a full scholarship to the business school at the University of New Mexico where he hoped to learn enough "to become a millionaire by the time I was forty." But shortly before he went off to college, he had a vision, "complete with music and singing," that told him he was to have a lifetime helping the poor instead. "I realized I'd have to give up girls and dancing and booze and become a kind of monk." His local pastor refused to support his vocation, telling him he was a *parandero,* the lowest sort of drunken bum. Father Cassidy went on to the seminary anyway, studied theology "until it came out my ears," and decided to become a priest.

By the time John Collier arrived in Peñasco, Father Cassidy had managed to involve himself in most aspects of community life. To help start a clinic, he organized a fund-raising bazaar and did much of the construction labor for the clinic himself. "It was the fulfillment of my vision," he says. He attended meetings of the Soil Conservation Service to argue for better soil erosion control and year-round maintenance of the acequias. He advised Hispanic people how to get small loans for feed and livestock and how to introduce more nitrogen into their worn-out soil. Frequently, when people got sick, he drove them to the Peñasco clinic himself. Father Cassidy had always loved science, especially atomic theory and inorganic chemistry, so when the local high school chemistry teacher was drafted, Father Cassidy stepped in and taught the class for the remainder of the year. He became involved with the local Boy Scout troop and took them on trips into the mountains where, a few years earlier, he'd taught himself to ski. In his spare time, he carved wooden statues and played the guitar, ukelele, piano, and accordian. (In his youth, he had played with a country music band.) During his short tenure in Peñasco, he became the most popular priest that the valley ever had. But his work did not end there.

When electricity was about to enter the Mora Valley, thirty miles north of Peñasco, Father Cassidy persuaded people along the thirty-five-mile route to grant the right-of-way to the REA

(Rural Electric Association). Then, realizing that most people were too poor to afford the hook-up fee, he acquired his electrician's license and connected hundreds of houses for free.

"I was not too popular in some circles," he says, recalling how the archbishop questioned his participation in the construction of a non-denominational clinic. "I said to him, 'Excellency, even non-Catholics get sick.'" Though the REA frowned on his performing free labor, it permitted him to work for the poor anyway.

Collier photographed the popular priest in every aspect of his work. Roy Stryker sent these photographs, along with those taken of general community life, to the United States Information Agency, which included them in a brochure aimed at offsetting the pro-Nazi movement among the politically torn people of South America. In the brochure, Las Trampas was depicted as an ideal Hispanic community whose members worked together for the common good, assisted by their young, energetic priest. He was portrayed as a political and economic force, as well as a member of the clergy, a deadly combination as far as the church was concerned. From halfway around the world, superiors began calling for his resignation.

"It was March 2, 1943," he recalls. "I got a call from the archbishop telling me I had to report the next day to Pecos. He had gotten his orders from the Holy Office to remove me. I was accused of being a communist." He roars with laughter; now, the incident seems absurd.

Although he never saw any evidence to prove his suspicions, Father Cassidy believes that the archbishop of Lima, Peru, might have been pro-Nazi, as some of the Catholic hierarchy were at the time. Traditional Catholics hold all Jews responsible for the death of Christ; the Nazi extermination program of Jews in the death camps only strengthened the Catholic argument that Jews would be punished for their sin. According to Father Cassidy, the archbishop of Peru considered the brochure as communist propaganda, thus contrary to the authoritarian goals of the church. He also felt the priest had become too involved in the lives of his parishioners, thereby weakening the church's position that clergy remain separate from laity except in matters of faith. The archbishop complained to the Vatican, which then contacted its apostolic delegate in Washington. Before long, orders were sent to the archbishop of Santa Fe to remove Father Cassidy from his parish. "The archbishop

Above: Father Cassidy finds time to teach a high school chemistry class. Peñasco, 1943. John Collier, Jr.
LC-USW 3-15274-C

Right: A Penitente cross marks a stop on the Good Friday pilgrimage. The Sangre de Cristo Mountains in the background were part of the Las Trampas land grant in 1751. Truchas, 1943. John Collier, Jr.
LC-USW 3-13703-C

[of Lima] saw America touted as a hotbed of communist activity," he says, his eyes twinkling. "And here I was in the middle of it. I looked like a Russian anyway. So they removed me. I had until the following morning to gather up my things and get out." He had been in his parish exactly seven months before he was exiled to Pecos on the eastern side of the mountains.

An interesting footnote to the story is that the archbishop died of apoplexy the very night he removed Father Cassidy from Peñasco. "I am a Catholic," Father Cassidy says when asked if he thinks this was biblical justice. "I don't believe in Old Testament vengeance."

The Hispanic villages of northern New Mexico belong to another century, another culture. They are enduring testimonials to the state's stormy colonial period; at the same time they are evidence of an ongoing struggle to survive the harsh facts of poverty and encroachment. Tucked away in the high, remote valleys in the rugged chain of the Sangre de Cristo Mountains, the villages of Las Trampas, El Valle, Rodarte, Chamisal, Peñasco, Ojo Sarco, Las Truchas, and Chimayo are shrouded in myth and legend, superstition and customs that date back to the Spain of Cervantes. Even today, some people speak a Spanish dialect deriving from that time.

In this part of New Mexico, about an hour's drive from Santa Fe, time seems arrested somewhere around the early eighteenth century. One

87

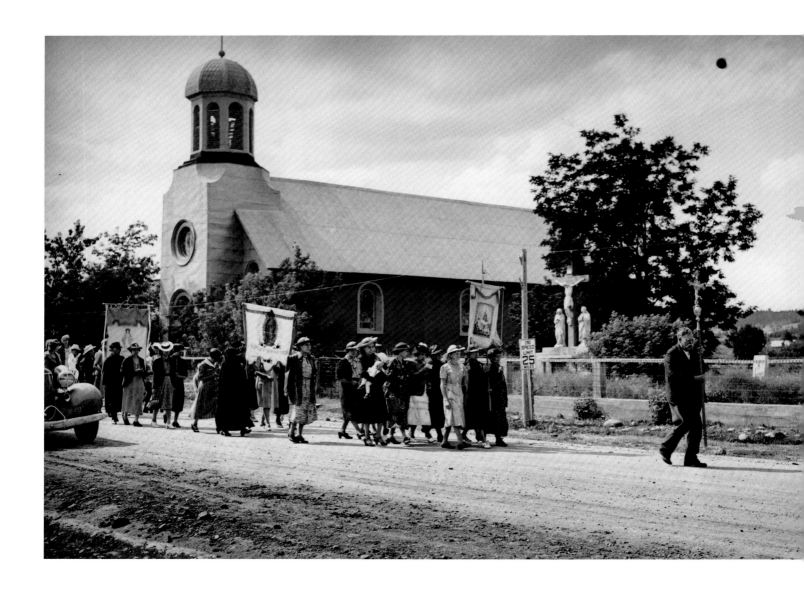

feels it on the winding roads from Española or Dixon, as one climbs from the sun-blasted sandstone hills to the cool, dark ponderosa forests that blanket the mountains. Here lie beauty and solitude; here, too, continuity is evidenced in three and four generations of the same family living in the adobe villages of their ancestors. A simple, dignified faith is evident everywhere. All over the piñon-studded hillsides, tiny shrines and chapels are reminders of the depth of religious belief here. For more than two centuries, the Spanish people of northern New Mexico have gone to these shrines to pray and to leave offerings to Jesus, the Virgin Mary, and their patron saints, including the Santo Niño, said to go about in the night, curing the sick and assuring the fertility of crops, animals, and women. When the saint's baby shoes wear out, people

buy him new ones and leave them at a chapel constructed in his honor at Chimayo.

Along the winding roads, simple white crosses, adorned with plastic flowers, are bleak memorials to loved ones killed here. Solitary wooden crosses, some of them ten feet high, mark stations along the way to the shrine at Chimayo. Every year, thousands of pilgrims join in a Good Friday procession to the santuario, whose sacred earth is believed to have miraculous healing powers. The Hispanic people are connected from birth to a strong Catholic faith that transcends the banality of lives caught up in mortgage payments, food stamps, and the repossession of trucks and washing machines.

"*Solo Dios basta,*" they say. Only God is enough. With faith they believe they can overcome the cruelty that has robbed them of their

Above: A religious procession, led by Facudo Medina, marches down the main street. Peñasco, 1940. Russell Lee. LC-USF 34-37147-D

Right: A farm family. Chamisal, 1940. Russell Lee. LC-USF 34-37007-D

lands and now threatens a way of life with roots deep in the soil, the community, and the rich comfort of families so large and extended that people simply call each other *primo* (cousin). "We are all related," one man from El Valle said, "so what does it matter, these names?"

The steadily encroaching Anglo culture has brought with it drastic shifts in social patterns and family roles in Las Trampas as well as in other northern New Mexico villages. The old agrarian barter system, vital to economic survival for three centuries, is now all but gone. Under this system, a farmer might go into a grocery store and trade a sheep for coffee, lard, and shoes. However, the needs of his family often exceeded his ability to pay. As his debt grew, the farmer would put up five or ten acres of family-held land. Eventually, the store foreclosed and the family lost its land. At this point, farmers were driven to find jobs as sheepherders or miners as far away as Colorado or Wyoming. Long separations from their families created yet new burdens.

Today, only a few old men, backs stooped from generations of hard labor, still patiently till the soil, coaxing crops of squash, beans, and corn at altitudes of 7,000 feet and higher. The younger generation, lured by the promise of jobs in the cities, is moving away at an alarming rate, leaving a gap in family structure as well as in traditional village networks. Those who remain are caught between a sense of obligation toward their families and the reality of having to make a living elsewhere.

Frank Lopez, who lives in Las Trampas with his wife and five children, commutes four hours a day to his job as a carpenter in Los Alamos. He prefers to live in his ancestral village because "my roots are here." This young man does not have time to raise crops or animals, nor does he want to. "My wife buys what we need in town," he says, "and my relatives give us stuff from their gardens."

Ordinary farmland which sold for as little as fifty dollars an acre twenty years ago, now fetches as much as $5,000 an acre. Families become divided in bitter feuds over the sale of ancestral lands to outsiders. Old people speculate about what will happen when they are gone and outsiders move in, bringing with them the habits and the hardware of the Anglo world.

An uncertain future, persistent poverty, loss of ancestral lands, and many men's long absences from their families have all contributed to a general malaise that grips residents of northern New Mexico villages. But there is another element at

work here, the result of isolation and inbreeding. Jealousy and gossip often undermine a traditional village network of trust; whole families become divided over something as petty as where a fence line should go. Battles over water rights frequently have bizarre consequences. Once, in a village near Española, a local farmer was accused of improperly diverting water from an acequia. The mayordomo, in charge of the ditch and its rights, cut off the farmer's flow. They fought, first with hoes, then hand to hand, and at last the mayordomo bit off the farmer's ear. When the farmer took the matter to court, the mayordomo was acquitted.

Within the villages, an undercurrent of desperation often erupts in lethal arguments in local cantinas or at home. In Truchas, during the thirties, a man shot his neighbor through the heart over possession of a can of beer. Another deliberately drove his car off a cliff, with his girlfriend strapped to the seat. As one elderly man said bitterly, "We as a people are turned against ourselves. The greatness that God intended for us will never be ours for we are too busy devouring each other."

Today the Hispanic villages of northern New Mexico are trying to hang on. Communities seek ways to preserve old buildings, customs, and the priceless art work of their churches. While the culture is undergoing drastic change, there is continuity and caring. It is reflected in the faces of those who have lived here all their lives, clinging to land, community, church, and family. What else is there, they ask? *Lo que ne puede remediar, hay que aquantar,"* they say. What cannot be remedied must be endured.

The Hispanic people know much about endurance. They have been in this area for nearly three hundred years, pitting themselves against their harsh environment. Claimed in 1598 by Don Juan de Oñate, the territory was a rugged expanse of mountains and deserts where "heathen savages" roamed. In the name of the Roman pope, native Indians were forced into servitude and Catholicism and gave up most of their lands to loyal patrons of the king. Resentful of the Spaniards who disrupted every aspect of their lives, the Pueblo tribes banded together in 1680 and drove at least 2,500 colonists clear to El Paso and killed 400 of them, including most of their harsh Franciscan masters. All things Spanish were destroyed—churches, haciendas, artifacts, and fortresses. Twelve years later, Don Diego de Vargas reclaimed the territory and permanent settlement began. The period of reconquest, though frequently bloody, paved the way for a

Above: Alfresco art. Amalia, 1943. John Collier, Jr. LC-USW 3-18014-C

Right: José Lopez rides from his hacienda in Rodarte to the mercado in Peñasco, 1940. Russell Lee. LC-USF 34-37142-D

viable Hispanic culture, apparent in the architecture, customs, language, and traditions of today.

During Spanish colonial times, both stubbornness and the will to survive were crucial to maintaining the barest sort of a life in a territory far removed from civilization. By the beginning of the nineteenth century, all of New Mexico was still a perilous frontier, with most villages fending for themselves. The crown was largely indifferent to the plight of the colony for it held little of economic value. There was no gold, only the souls of the Indians to be systematically collected, like trophies. The restless Spaniards, desiring riches, staked out villages and moved on. Except in the larger cities of Santa Fe and Albuquerque, education was unknown, and a parish priest visited about once a year. Even then, few could afford the money he charged for his services. Dispensations had to go through the bishop of Durango, Mexico, 1,500 miles away, and often took years. Cut off from their cultural roots in Spain and Mexico, the Hispanos of northern New Mexico began to improvise, especially in matters of religion.

La Hermandad de Nuestro Padre Jesus Nazareno, the Penitente Brotherhood, came into being at the end of the eighteenth century to fill the vacuum left by the clergy; they said rosaries, conducted burials, cared for the sick, consoled bereaved families, kept up the yearly cycles of feasts and festivals with improvised ceremonies, maintained law and order, and enforced good conduct with threat of punishments of their own. In these isolated villages, the Penitentes were for many years the only civil or religious authority. They wove a tight web of interdependence that drew people together.

During their long years of isolation from the rest of New Mexico and the world, Hispanic men depended even more deeply upon the brotherhood and found solace in the mysteries of the cofradia. Although the church orthodoxy attempted to destroy their authority in individual villages, and for a time outlawed them, the Penitentes—pious, humble, strict, and unrelenting—never submitted. They simply went underground, many of them moving their moradas away from town and conducting their rituals in utmost secrecy. For more than a century, the brotherhood helped to unify remote Hispanic villages and reinforced cultural pride; for many years they were also a strong political force which could make or break any local election.

Not until 1947 were the Penitentes officially accepted as a legitimate arm of the Roman Catholic church. In most villages of northern New Mexico they are still a force, but their numbers have been severely reduced in recent years. In many cofradias, a surprising number of young men join, seeing the brotherhood as a way to combat the effects of the dominant Anglo culture as well as a means to reinforce their own Hispanic pride. In the Taos area, three moradas have a combined membership of more than two hundred men. Here, as elsewhere, the brotherhood serves an important function during Lent as well as at other times of the year. They distribute food to the poor, hold wakes, comfort the bereaved, and settle disputes among members and their families. While the Penitentes are still a vital part of Hispanic culture, few men admit to their non-Hispanic friends to being members, fearing loss of what little privacy they have left.

Nearly every Hispanic-surnamed resident of northern New Mexico claims to be a descendant of those colonists who first arrived with Vargas. Manuel "Rudy" Pacheco II of Taos can trace his ancestry on his mother's side to Nicolás Ortiz, a conquistador who arrived from Guevara, Spain, in 1692. Pacheco's father's family were surveyors and mappers of El Camino Real during Vargas's time; one of his descendants, José Antonio Salazar y Pacheco, mapped the Escalante Trail all the way to Salt Lake City in 1776. Pacheco's wife, Angelica, is a descendant of Antonio Martínez de Godoi, a grantee of Arroyo Seco in the early eighteenth century. Such lineage is important to all Hispanic families who wish to pass on a sense of historical continuity to their children. Luis Torres of Arroyo Seco is a fifty-four-year-old rancher who looks as if he could have ridden up the Rio Grande with Vargas. He lives in the same old adobe house in which he was born and raises Charolais cattle. Some of his land has been in the family for generations, but through his own efforts he has increased his holdings tenfold. "I am land poor," he says, "but I am happy in my world."

This is not an Anglo world, nor an Indian world, but one with roots deep in Old Spain and Old Mexico; it is one of courtesy, devotion, hard work, and something the natives call *verguenza*—a combination of traditions, customs, and personal integrity. A man with *verguenza* acts fairly with his fellow man and does not cheat him; he works hard at his job, whether it's for a dollar a day or five dollars an hour. To become *sin verguenza* is to betray one's knowledge, customs, and loyalty for material gain—for example, a man who sells his land to Anglos, becomes a tool

Right: A Penitente cross. Taos, 1943. John Collier, Jr. LC-USW 3-13760-C

Above: Onofre Leyba Vigil, who lived to be ninety-eight years old. Las Trampas, 1943. John Collier, Jr.
LC-USW 3-17803-E

Left: Salomon Ortega delivers mail in this light buggy. Peñasco, 1940. Russell Lee.
LC-US

Right: A boy standing in front of a picture representing "balanced" farm life, such as does not exist in this part of the country. Peñasco, 1943. John Collier, Jr.
LC-USW 3-14640-C

of politicos, or pursues a career in law, banking, or commerce.

A rebellion of sorts has taken place in recent years as more and more Hispanos see education as the only means to have a stronger voice in state and national government or in getting well-paying jobs in the cities. Yet to the older generation, many of whom are illiterate, such goals are *sin verguenza.* The contradiction places many ambitious young Hispanics in a dilemma, for advancing themselves often means jeopardizing their positions in ancestral villages or even in their families. Said one elderly man in Rodarte, who has seen several of his children become important figures in the state bureaucracy, *"El arbol que crece torcido, nunca su rama enderza"* (If the tree grows crooked, you can't expect the branches to grow straight), meaning that the younger generation can't pass *verguenza* on to their children when they themselves have betrayed it.

One example of *verguenza* occurred in 1986 when the people of Las Trampas got together to replaster and refurbish the two-hundred-year-old church of San José de Gracia, the center of village life. For six months, hundreds of volunteers mixed adobe, plastered from high scaffolds erected inside the church, and carefully removed the santos, bultos, and reredos made by their ancestors. A spirit of cooperation joined everyone together; families who had not spoken to one another in years found a new connection as cracks and holes in the old adobe walls began to disappear through their efforts. Food was provided, free of charge, by village women; construction was supervised by village elders. Small children helped by dropping tiny armloads of straw or pouring toy buckets of water into troughs of wet mud. "We did it ourselves," says Bernie Lopez, the thirty-four-year-old mayordoma, who raised $8,000 through donations to pay for repairs, including a new roof. "No money came from the state or federal government." The work so united the people of Las Trampas that when Mrs. Lopez announced plans to replaster the outside walls the following year, half of the population signed up. For the people of Las Trampas, the church is their center of devotion as well as a symbol of their tenacious longevity.

Las Trampas has not changed much since John Collier made his memorable photographic study there in 1943. The town lies in the gentle valley of the Trampas River that winds through the meadows south of town. New Mexico State Highway 76 connects Las Trampas to Peñasco, Chamisal, Truchas, Chimayo, and to the larger

Left: Cleofas Lopez, said to be the best enjaradora *around, smoothes out the plaster with her hands. Chamisal, 1940. Russell Lee.*
LC-USF 33-12811-M5

Right: Las Trampas is an eighteenth-century Hispanic village which was once a sheep-raising center. Because of overgrazing and loss of community lands, inhabitants now work as migratory laborers and at subsistence farming, 1943. John Collier, Jr.
LC-USW 3-14644-C

world beyond, though it is paved now, without the ruts that John Collier remembers. The rugged Sangre de Cristos, snow covered seven months of the year, rise to the east, a spectacular chain of mountains that have both protected and defined the village more than two hundred years. At 8,000 feet, Las Trampas is remote and secluded; an air of mystery and timelessness hangs over the quiet plaza and the adobe houses that dot the hillsides. There is still no gas station, convenience store, or fast-food restaurant in Las Trampas, only the church and a few houses on the plaza. A few house trailers add an incongruous note. The elementary school, where John Collier photographed rural education as it was in 1943, has been closed for nearly three decades; a school bus hauls a handful of local children to the consolidated school at Peñasco. Meadows dense with chokecherries and willows lie on both sides of the river; horses graze in verdant hay meadows. An ancient aqueduct carries water to old, hand-dug acequias, and crisscrosses the land in deep veins. Here as in other Hispanic villages, history is evident everywhere—in old buildings and wall murals, sagging hand-hewn fences, and apple orchards falling to neglect because no one cares for them anymore. Pitch-roofed adobe houses, some of them two hundred years old, stand beneath aged cottonwood trees, affectionately called *los abuelos*—the grandfathers. Only about one hundred people are left in Las Trampas, and they are mostly older people, steeped in myth and legend, superstitions and customs.

Las Trampas was founded in 1751 when Gov-

ernor Tomás Velez Cachupín granted 14,065 acres to twelve families who named it Santo Tomás Apostol del Río de Las Trampas. These early colonists were partly Spanish and partly a mixture of Mexican Indian. To them, the land must have seemed forbidding, with its vastness, mystery, and danger all around. The rugged Sangre de Cristos were unexplored, part of a wilderness that belonged to the Picuris Indians whose pueblo lay about ten miles west. The Indians, friendly at first, began to demand horses and food. When the nervous Tramperos wrote to the governor, requesting a few muskets to supplement their meagre arsenal of bows, arrows, and lances, they were denied. Weapons were needed elsewhere. The Tramperos were on their own.

The twelve original families, all related to their leader, sixty-year-old Juan de Arguello, made the most of their environment. They cleared the land a little bit at a time and planted crops; a few scrawny goats and sheep nibbled the dry grass. Gathering their courage, a handful of small yet sturdy men, religious and untiring, went up into the mountains. They cut down trees for houses, corrals, and firewood. They built an adobe village, fortified by a wall, and constructed a church thirty varas long, including transept. Local artisans carved santos and painted reredos and bultos; the church gained fame as the most beautiful one around.

By 1776, the population of Las Trampas had increased to sixty-three families; the population was 278. In a report issued to the Holy Office in Madrid, the parish priest, who visited about once a month, offered this assessment of his flock: They are "a ragged lot . . . festive as they are poor, and very merry. Accordingly, most of them are low class, and there are very few of good, or even moderately good, blood . . . in general they speak . . . bad Spanish. . . ."

Nonetheless, a community evolved. But raids against the Tramperos continued by the Plains Indians and the Picuris. Once, legend has it, the outnumbered Tramperos were huddled inside the walls of the plaza, waiting for a large band of Indians to finish them off. Suddenly, two old people appeared at the gate. They waited for the Indians to ride up, then raised their hands. The

Opposite: The one-room Ojo Sarco school has eight grades and two teachers. Textbooks are from the public school system of Michigan and have little relation to Hispanic culture. The ABC's, penmanship, and grammar are taught on the blackboard. Most of the teaching is in Spanish, the language spoken in the children's homes, and as a result students such as these rarely speak English fluently. Ojo Sarco, 1943. John Collier, Jr.
LC-USW 3-14517-E

Right: The general store and post office serves as a popular meeting place. Left to right: Eduardo Vigil, Jacobo Romero, Bernabe Leyba, an unidentified man, Avenado Sanchez, and Pacomio Romero exchange the news of the day in front of the wood stove. Las Trampas, 1943. John Collier, Jr.
LC-USW 3-15246-C

Indians retreated. The old couple, according to legend, was none other than Mary and Joseph.

The isolated village, poor, deeply religious, and immersed in an expanding culture, continued to survive. Villagers gathered a pharmacopoeia of natural herbs and medicines to help them through generations when no medical help was available. In the late eighteenth century, a woman's expected lifespan was no more than forty years; for men it was less than fifty. Half of the children in any given family died before their third birthdays and were buried in tiny wooden coffins, handcarved by grieving male relatives. At that altitude, winter came early and snow lay on the ground six and seven months of the year; sometimes, a killing frost struck as early as August, destroying essential crops. Families ate one meal a day, usually nothing more than tortillas or a mush made from corn meal. They learned to forage for nuts and berries and to make tea out of roots and bark. Wild game was scarce, and the few domestic animals they had brought with them were devoured during lean years. Indians frequently kidnapped women and children to trade to other tribes for guns and horses. Life here was so difficult that some of the original families soon left.

For those who remained, the ejido, land held in common by the village, was of vital importance in maintaining a subsistence economy. By long tradition rather than written law, colonists took for themselves no more than five or ten acres on which to grow crops. The land that was left—unfenced and undisputed—was used according to need. Sheep, goats, and cattle all grazed on the vast tract that began at the top of 12,200-foot Trampas Peak, went down through lush meadows and stands of towering ponderosas, across creeks, and swept up into the semiarid foothills.

When the Americans took over New Mexico under the Treaty of Guadalupe Hidalgo in 1848, life began to change. Under this treaty the United States paid Mexico $15 million for land now comprising the states of California, Nevada, and Utah, and parts of Arizona, New Mexico, Colorado, and Wyoming. By the terms of Guadalupe Hidalgo, the American government agreed to respect all land grants that had been made by the Spanish and American government for the preceding 200 years and to place in the public domain the remaining ungranted areas.

This provision unleashed a wave of fraud, bloodshed, and chicanery unequaled in the nation's history. The Mexican government scrambled to issue land grants to favored Mexican citi-

Above: Gomasinda Martínez washing wool in the creek. Chamisal, 1940. Russell Lee. LC-USF 33-12817-M5

Right: A boy chases his family's cow and calf along the irrigation ditch. Peñasco, 1940. Russell Lee. LC-USF 33-12864-MI

Overleaf: The town of Rodarte and the surrounding mountains were part of the original Las Trampas land grant in 1751, 1940. Russell Lee. LC-USF 34-37224-D

zens who could then sell the land, at their
personal profit, to greedy American speculators.
Court records in these western states show that,
in nearly every case, these grants were made as
bribes. Fraudulent surveys were then presented to
American officials as "proof" of ownership of vast
tracts of land in New Mexico.

For example, in 1768, Ignacio Cháves and
others had petitioned the Spanish crown for
approximately 10,000 acres, an amount increased
by fraudulent survey to 243,036 acres. The
Estancia Mexican grant, restricted by Mexican
law to 48,708 acres, was enlarged by fraudulent
survey to 415,036 acres. In case after case, original land grant claims were enlarged five to fifty
times. Millions of additional acres were awarded
through forgery; it was a real estate free-for-all
that lasted well into the twentieth century.

In nearly every case, the majority of grants
wrested from the Hispanic people consisted of
their community property—the ejidos. Without
them, the simple, land-based economy could not

survive. In village after village, the economy col-
lapsed as hard-pressed citizens tried to wring a
subsistence living from five or ten acres of fam-
ily-owned land. But much of this was soon lost
as the American government imposed property
taxes, posting the notices in English which few
Hispanics could read or understand. Before long,
thousands of acres were lost through default. By
the early years of the century, one man in four
was forced to seek work outside his village. Some
became sheepherders, railroad workers, miners,
and stoop laborers, so called because they were
forced to use *el cortito,* a short hoe which turned
strong workers into hunched men, plagued by
back problems all their lives.

At first, as other ejidos were gobbled up, it
seemed that the Tramperos would keep theirs
intact. A government survey in 1893 even
increased the size of the original grant to about
28,000 acres, more than double its original size.
For the 1,500 or so settlers then on the land, it
seemed that the United States government was

truly on their side. They continued their hard-working pastoral existence, but not for long.

According to noted southwestern historian William de Buys, whose book *Enchantment and Exploitation: The Life and Hard Times of a New Mexico Mountain Range* focuses on this important episode, one man brought about the downfall of the Las Trampas ejido. In 1900, a disgruntled Trampero named David Martínez, Jr., sued for partition of the Las Trampas Grant. As a descendant of one of the twelve original families, he claimed the largest single interest, about 18 percent, which he hoped to sell to pay off outstanding debts. As a result of his patrimony, a district judge soon ordered the sale of the entire ejido; it brought eighteen cents an acre at a public sale held without the knowledge or consent of the other residents of the grant. By the time they found out, it was too late.

A tangle of legal maneuvers lasted until 1903, at which time the grant was sold for the second time, at sixty cents an acre to Frank Bond, an Española sheepman and merchant who had plans to log the whole vast acreage. It soon turned out that Bond owned more than just the ejido; he had purchased 1,500 acres of privately owned land as well, including houses and farms occupied by bewildered Hispanos threatened with removal. Only fifty acres had been spared.

One man, Juan B. Ortega, who lived in El Valle, just a few miles from Las Trampas, desperately fought to save his people and their confiscated lands. He waged a lengthy and costly legal battle that eventually returned more than a thousand acres to Las Trampas residents, who were each required to sign quitclaims, at a dollar apiece, to their interest in the commons. Though the settlement was the best that Ortega could negotiate with the much-hated Bond, his own people criticized him as the traitor who "sold away the grant." Many believe that the deed to their commons was issued to Bond a full seven years before Ortega took up the cause on their behalf. Many also believe that Ortega pocketed most of the money paid for the ejido and distributed only a fraction to his neighbors. In Las Trampas and the surrounding area Ortega is still bitterly regarded as the worst sort of example of *sin verguenza*. In Hispanic villages, old grievances die hard.

Following the loss of Las Trampas ejido, privately owned lands averaging only three or four acres each became tragically overgrazed. According to the Tewa Basin Study released by the federal government in 1936, villagers were forced

to feed cactus to their stock to keep them alive. Even so, a number of horses and cattle starved during the hard winter of 1934–35 when more than twenty feet of snow fell on the community. Because of nearly two hundred years of overuse, farmland was generally poor, and many acequias were inadequate to supply the necessary irrigation. Some vegetables were grown on the badly depleted land, but the main crop was wheat because "they must at least make certain of their bread." The report concluded that the number of people in the area was five times greater than the land could support.

Moreover, the Tewa Basin Study found that artisans such as weavers and carvers, trying desperately to support their families, were exploited by dealers. A good weaver earned no more than a dollar a day making blankets and rugs that retailed for hundreds of dollars. The largest industries in the area were tie-making and lumbering; workers bartered their products for food rather than receiving wages. "Cash is very scarce," the report said, with residents heavily in debt to local grocery stores who eventually refused to give them any more credit. When this happened, families went on relief or tried to barter for what they could. One old Cordova man is said to have exchanged his only pair of shoes for a pound of coffee and some lard.

The Tewa Basin Study revealed that although

Opposite: Part of the Tewa Basin, 1935. Dorothea Lange.
LC-USF 34-18337-C

Above: Benjamin Dominguez coming out of his fruit storage cellar. Chamisal, 1940. Russell Lee. LC-USF 34-37022-D

Right: Felipita and Salomon Dominguez, a fifth-grade teacher at the Las Trampas school, prepare fruit for canning. Chamisal, 1940. Russell Lee. LC-USF 34-37098-D

nearly all drinking water was hauled from irrigation ditches, where livestock also watered, no typhoid cases were reported. Infant mortality and childbirth death rates were high. The study decried the lack of medical facilities and urged public health participation, a suggestion that New Dealers accepted and implemented by starting clinics at Peñasco and Questa, both photographed by John Collier in 1943.

Despite local insistence that "we always eat well," the Tewa Basin Study reported that "at the present time 20 to 90 percent of the children are undernourished, and a large percentage of the population suffers from malnutrition." Years of overgrazing and drought, coupled with the constant subdividing of family acreage after the loss of the ejidos, resulted in a land base no longer capable of supporting farm animals. The animals that were left, the study said, were "literally skin and bones."

Seventy-year-old Ofelia Lopez of Las Trampas remembers those times of *poquito* well. For years the family had no animals, except chickens, and very little food. They lived on tortillas and beans; Ofelia made clothing from flour sacks.

Sometimes she dug for roots, gathered wild berries and nuts, and "prayed to God to help us." Ofelia Lopez is a simple woman, solid and large-boned, the mother of eight children, including twins born when she was almost fifty years old. She and her husband, Fernando, survived the thirties because he, like so many men of the valley, went away to work when agriculture was no longer able to sustain them. Every two weeks, he sent home forty or fifty dollars. In 1943, a mine explosion left Fernando totally blind. He could never work again. At first he could not get workman's compensation, but then Dennis Chavez, a powerful New Mexico senator, stepped in to help them. Welfare payments soon amounted to twenty-eight dollars a month, and the family survived on that for many years. Fernando owned an acre of land, and "we grew a little food." But one day, the blind old miner, desperate for money, borrowed five dollars from his cousin, Ferminia Leyba. For many years, until she got old, Ferminia was the local curandera who used herbs and other medicines to make people well. She was the nearest thing to a doctor that Las Trampas ever had. When Fernando couldn't pay

Left: A small child washing her face in one corner of her home. Taos County, 1939. Russell Lee. LC-SF 34-34234-D

Above right: Making tortillas. Taos County, 1939. Russell Lee. LC-USF 34-34220-D

back the loan, Ferminia took the land, even though there was no signed paper between them.

Ofelia Lopez settles in her chair, gazing out the window at her chickens scratching in the yard. "So after that, we had to use other people's land." She bears no grudge toward Doña Ferminia for their reduced circumstances because the old curandera is still part of their family.

The Lopezes are the largest and most prominent family group in Las Trampas, so intertwined and intermarried that "we call each other *primo* [cousin], even if we're not related," says Filia Lopez, an aunt of Ofelia's. She is sixty-nine years old and has borne eleven children, the first when she was seventeen, the last when she was forty. Nine survived. Pictures of the six boys and three girls are prominently displayed in her high-ceilinged living room, along with old photographs of long-dead relatives, shrines to the Virgin Mary and to Jesus, and a plaque commemorating fifty years of marriage to her husband, Tranquilino, in 1984. There are other pictures too, of twenty-eight grandchildren and ten great-grandchildren, proof of a rich and meaningful life.

Filia Lopez was born just over the hill in Ojo Sarco but came to Las Trampas as an infant to be reared by an aunt when her mother died. She cared for sheep, goats, cows, and a large garden and learned to make soap and to can and dry food raised on the premises. Even today she cards and spins her own wool, weaves blankets and rugs on an old loom that belonged to her grandmother, makes quilts out of old scraps from her sewing, and cans or freezes her own food from a large garden below the house. Nothing goes to waste. Filia Lopez is a prime example of *mujerota,* which means that she has fulfilled the highest ideals of bearing and rearing many children, as well as running her household and doing her share of raising food and livestock for her family.

Eighty-seven-year-old Tranquilino Lopez is a short, wiry man with strong arms and hands developed during long years of labor as a mucker in the zinc and copper mines. He is still handsome, with a full head of dark hair and deep-set, inquisitive eyes. Despite a lifetime of hardship, Tranquilino has a ready smile, and he tells numerous stories which are invariably jokes on himself. He was born in the same rambling adobe house where he has lived all his life. His father and grandfather were born here too, adding on more rooms as their families expanded. Like his neighbors, Tranquilino also went outside to work, first in the mines, then for the Denver and Rio Grande Western Railroad where he helped to lay track. During the war, he worked briefly as a janitor at Los Alamos, for fifty cents an hour. He did not like the work, however, and soon returned to the mines.

For seven months a year he worked underground, 163 days at a time, Sundays included; his only days off were Christmas and the Fourth of July. He received, at the height of his mining career in 1947, $4.50 for an eight-hour day. The family of eleven managed to live on ninety dollars a month. The former miner/railroad worker came home during the spring planting months, then returned to his job in the fall. Of the long separations from his family, he says, "She stay here all right, and I go there all right. Nothing the matter with that. We all survive plenty good." His laughter is rich and hearty. He is not given to complaint about what his life might have been; rather, he tells of how his family stuck together, inspired by his absence. Tranquilino Lopez exhibits not *macho,* which in this part of the country refers to the behavior of a mule, but *hombria,* performing long and difficult labor for the sake of his family. Through this dedication, a man achieves a form of independence that is akin to *el estilo antigua,* living the old way. Yet this was not always possible, even for a man this strong-willed.

Tranquilino Lopez was once forced to go on welfare, after a mine accident incapacitated him in 1955. The family received thirty dollars a month, an insult to his pride. "Every month, somebody come," he says. "How much money you got? How many people live here? So after a while, to hell with it. So much trouble for so little money. So I had to find another way." Ever since then he has survived on workman's compensation and social security. For more than thirty years, he has tended his apple orchard as well as a two-acre garden plot below the house, "so we have plenty to eat all the time."

Tranquilino's long absences made her strong, Filia says. "I had to be mother, father, everything. Inside, I took care of the house. Outside, the animals and garden. On Saturdays, we took the wagon and went up in the mountains for wood. Even the little ones helped." During lean years, she and the children gathered piñon nuts and carried them in sacks to the mercantile at Truchas, hoping "we would get enough to buy shoes."

Across the highway from Tranquilino and Filia lives Juan Antonio Lopez, Tranquilino's older brother, who is ninety years old. Juan Lopez was photographed, along with his late wife, Maclovia, and six of his ten children, by John Collier in 1943. This was a happy time, he says, when Maclovia was still alive, but after she died in 1967, things have not been good. Unlike Tranquilino, there is no joy or anticipation in this lonely, brittle man who spends most of his days resting in a darkened room. He gets up briefly to welcome a visitor and says he remembers how "Juan Collie-year" slept right there on the kitchen floor, while making his two-week-long study "in January when everything is frozen." The old man manages to smile a little; he is frail and weak, the color of old parchment. He says his family thought it peculiar that the government would want pictures of them, but they obliged. These were the photographs that

Below: Maclovia Lopez spins wool from the family sheep in the evenings when her children are in bed. Las Trampas, 1943. John Collier, Jr.
LC-USW 3-17814-E

Right: Juan and Maclovia Lopez have lived in Las Trampas all their lives, as have many generations of their family before them. Here the family eats a supper of tortillas, beans, and chili. Clockwise: Juan, Luissa, Luis, Pat, Maclovia, Victor, Liberato, and Manuelita, 1943. John Collier, Jr.
LC-USW 3-15237-C

Opposite: Young Luis Lopez helps his father haul water from the stream below the house. There is no electricity or plumbing, 1943. John Collier, Jr.
LC-USW 3–17887-C

Above: Juan and Maclovia look in the new Sears, Roebuck catalogue for a harness. Since it will cost sixty dollars, they will probably do without, 1943. John Collier, Jr.
LC-USW 3-17838-E

eventually caused Father Cassidy to be removed from his job.

Juan Lopez has not forgotten Collier's visit forty-five years ago. "He ate tortillas and beans with us," Juan Lopez says, nibbling at a pizza left over from lunch. "He haul water, break ice, chop wood. Everything." He brought small presents to Maclovia, too—a sack of potatoes, a jug of cider, candy for the children. The memory of the photographer's kindness evokes a rare smile from Juan Lopez. John Collier went to mass with the Lopez family. He became almost like a *manito*, or little brother. Through them, he gained unusual access to Hispanic village life and was able to photograph a culture that changed after the Second World War when returning servicemen brought new attitudes from an outside world. Indoor plumbing, electricity, and paved roads all came after the war. The traditional life photographed by Collier—horse-drawn wagons, one-room schools, and the last of a post-ejido barter economy soon vanished.

Juan Antonio Lopez also had to work outside of Las Trampas during the thirties, first as a sheepherder in Wyoming. He did not much like sheep, because "you have to watch them all the time, even when you sleep." At one time, his father was considered wealthy because he owned twenty acres, but when he died, the land was divided up among eight children. "Now nothing left for nobody," says the old don who is afraid that his children will fight over his house when he is gone. Such fears are common in this part of New Mexico where inheritances sometimes include a strip of land eighteen inches wide and half a mile long. One old man in Taos left one of his children half a bed and three chickens; another only a pair of shoes and a pitchfork.

Juan Lopez lives with his sixty-one-year-old daughter, Bertha. She is a small, birdlike woman who runs a clean, efficient house, tends the garden, and looks after her father the way her mother did. But fatigue engulfs her. She has had brain cancer and a stroke, and she suffers from heart disease. Long divorced from a Las Trampas sheepherder who was later found murdered in a Wyoming sheep camp, she says of her marriage, "It was not the thing to do, but Clarence was the best bet I had in my life. I had never even gone out on a date, so when he asked me to marry him, I was surprised." According to tradition, Clarence Vigil had to send a letter to Juan Lopez, then herding sheep in Wyoming, to ask for his permission to marry Bertha. "But he couldn't read, so I was a bride-to-be for three months until someone came along who could read it for him." The marriage lasted five years. "He was a drunk, just like my father said." According to Bertha Lopez Vigil, this is the only correct opinion her father ever had.

She says of him, "To tell you the truth, he was a very strict man. He never took us anywhere. All I remember is working, working, all of us working, along with my mother. It's what killed her, the work. She had ten children, she was the postmistress, and once, she even taught school." Bertha Lopez says it was her mother's income as postmistress that actually supported the family, so that her father only had to go away and work for seven years, first as a sheepherder, then for the state highway department, building roads.

She says he is a rich man, but stingy, and "I can't get anything out of him. Not even a dime." She claims his friends are few, he doesn't go to mass, and that he once was a Penitente but quit because "he couldn't get along with them. He can't get along with anyone, really."

Despite the fact that his wife briefly taught school in Las Trampas, Juan Lopez did not believe in education for his family. Only three of the Lopez children were allowed to finish high school; no matter how hard she tried, Maclovia

was unable to persuade her husband to change his mind about the rest of them. "A woman can never go against her husband," Bertha says. "It's not our way. The man's word was always final, and she had to accept it even when she knew he was wrong."

Bertha Lopez has tried to come to grips with the difficulties of her past; at the same time she tries to maintain a balance between her role within the village and her family life. Despite her physical limitations, she worked long hours on the 1986 church restoration project and plans to work on it again. On Good Fridays, she always makes the thirteen-mile pilgrimage to the santuario at Chimayo as a way of manifesting her deeply rooted Catholic faith. At home she cares not only for her elderly, ailing father but for her

two-year-old granddaughter as well, so that the child's mother can commute to her job in Santa Fe. She feeds her family from a large garden that she tends by herself, and distributes surplus vegetables to friends and relatives. Acceptance is part of her life.

"God has given me this life," she says. "It is not an entirely good life, but it is the only one I know."

Good Friday dawns clear and bright in Las Trampas where a spectacle nearly as old as the town is about to take place. First comes the *encuentro*—the last encounter between Holy Mother and Son. The whole town has turned out to watch the procession: the Penitentes, carrying two statues of the crucified Christ, one in purple, the other veiled in white, march out of the morada, singing the saddest of their alabados in voices that echo to the hills beyond. Every few yards, the Penitentes fall to the ground and kiss the hard, dry earth. There are less than twenty of them, ranging in age from about twelve to eighty. They are led by the blind old man Fernando Lopez. He is supported by two young men, one on either side, to catch him if he falls. But Don Fernando, his sightless eyes turned toward the warm sun, does not need assistance. With a string of rosary beads draped from his neck, he moves haltingly along the pathway, singing the old hymns from memory.

Another procession comes from the church, four women carrying a statue of the Virgin Mary on a platform. She is dressed in a black shawl; only a tiny, pinched face stares out at the crowd. She looks like Bertha Lopez, who is making the pilgrimage to Chimayo, seventeen miles away. Filia and Tranquilino Lopez, dressed in their best, march solemnly along with the faithful. Ofelia Lopez, clutching her rosary, nods as she follows the Virgin Mary slowly around the plaza. Tears roll down her cheeks; to most villagers, this solemn reenactment of Christ's passion is very real, an occasion to think about the sin, guilt, and redemption taught by the Catholic church. Two days hence on Easter, there will be joy and resurrection.

The old curandera Ferminia Leyba, who took the land belonging to Fernando Lopez, is there, too, dressed in a white lace mantilla. Though she is more than ninety years old, she is still beautiful, resembling a Velasquez painting. Because she is the oldest woman in Las Trampas, everyone makes way for her.

There is no need for a priest in this town

Opposite: Victor Lopez. Las Trampas, 1943. John Collier, Jr.
LC-USW 3-17993-C

Below: Luisa and Victor watch as Maclovia Lopez tends to her mending. Las Trampas, 1943. John Collier, Jr.
LC-USW 3-15213-C

today. The Penitentes perform this ritual, which they themselves invented and have varied only slightly throughout the centuries. Unlike similar ceremonies of the nineteenth century, there is no actual crucifixion, where the holiest man among them was selected to hang from the cross by means of leather thongs. There is not even a procession to the *calvario* anymore, only a small procession around the plaza.

The Penitentes look like the old wooden santos in the church—gaunt-eyed, hollow cheeked, eternally sad. Dressed mostly in jeans, dark shirts, and cowboy boots, all wear their rosaries around their necks and carry hymnals. They reach for a new and deeper level of meaning with these ancient alabados, first sung more than two hundred years ago when the church was new. Heads bowed, the two groups meet and the statue of Mary slowly embraces the statue of Jesus. A small girl, meant to represent the weeping Veronica, wipes the face of Jesus, as her scriptural counterpart did two thousand years ago. The girl holds up a hand towel, imprinted with the Holy Face. Then the people of Las Trampas kneel in the dirt and kiss the hem of the sacred garments of the two Cristos. When the group passes, the Penitentes go back to the morada, stopping every few yards to kneel and kiss the earth again.

The afternoon rosary is conducted by the Penitentes. The church is cold and damp; two wood stoves throw a ring of heat. When the rosary ends, the Penitentes file back to the morada, carrying the two statues of the Cristo. Another Cristo, a life-size one from the side altar, is placed on a catalfaque draped in black; twelve candles are lighted, then the black-clad statue of the Virgin Mary is turned to face the Cristo. Not a sound is heard until the Penitentes return, singing their alabados, this time so loudly that the sound vibrates throughout the old church and echoes into the plaza. The essence of what has kept the Hispanic villages alive for so many generations is here in this simple, elegant church, hallowed by more than two centuries of devotion.

The Good Friday services end when the Virgin Mary is taken to the morada, a small, windowless room about eight by twelve feet next to the church. Nothing suggests the fierce self-flagellation or bloodletting of both legend and practice; the room is filled with nothing but crucifixes, holy pictures, a statue of the Santo Niño, and the *carreta de la muerta*. The death figure is draped in black, his arrow of death drawn in his bow and aimed directly at the thigh of one of the Penitentes. In the old days, when the carreta was drawn around the plaza, the release of the arrow toward a villager meant that he or she would die soon. The Penitente sings on; the arrow stays in position.

When the service is finished, Felia and Tranquilino Lopez have a traditional Good Friday meal: *berdalaga* (a spinach-like wild vegetable), *tarega con sardinas* (eggs with sardines), frijoles, potatoes with cheese, and chili with sardines. Today, they do not eat meat. Today they think about their lives, their children, their village. Don Tranquilino walks outside and looks at his orchard and his fields. He sits under the *abuelo*— a cottonwood tree planted by his *tio* more than a century ago. He says he is like this tree, old and stubborn, and some day he will die, like the tree, like everything.

"No plant anymore," he says even though he's already put in his crops of peas and horse beans. "Too much work for an old man, eh?" His laughter is rich and deep as he leans back against the tree, the way he's done for more than eighty years. "Time for me to go to the *camposanto*. No use to get old."

With that, he gets up and swings his axe until he has chopped enough wood for Filia's stove. Then he goes to his acequia and cleans out some brush that has fallen across the ditch. In less than three weeks the water will start flowing again, on the first day of May, the way it has always done as far back as he can remember. Don Tranquilino wants to be ready, whenever the water comes. He notices that the willows and the cottonwoods are already starting to leaf out.

"Springtime always make me happy," he says. "Even underground. *No lloro, pero me acuerdo.* (I don't cry, but I remember.)"

Somehow, that is all that matters in the Hispanic villages of New Mexico.

Right: Grandfather Romero, the oldest man in Las Trampas, 1943. John Collier, Jr.
LC-USW 3-17877-C

CONCLUSION

While the New Deal in New Mexico was largely a failure, the work of the FSA photographers was not. Off and on during the eight-year period from 1935 to 1943 they depicted the heartland of the state, revealing an essential character heretofore unexplored. Most of this work was not the result of any direct assignment given by Roy Stryker but rather was the outcome of the photographers' own curiosity and response to the situations around them. These photographers were consummate risk takers, explorers in their own right; they faced discomfort and adversity as part of the job they set out to do. Long hours, low pay, tedious travel over dirt roads, and substandard accommodations only whetted their appetites to find out the human dimension of the depression and the early years of World War II.

The work of Dorothea Lange, Arthur Rothstein, Russell Lee, John Collier, and Jack Delano in New Mexico shows a rich blend of tradition, novelty, and cultural conflict as well as continuity. The photographs they made during this time are historical documents in themselves, to be examined again and again for clues to the past. What sorts of people lived here then? What do their faces reflect? Where was what Stryker called "the significant detail"—those cultural artifacts that reveal so much about the timeless character of a place? The photographs tell us much about New Mexico, yet they are universal statements too, steeped in the kind of human values that connect us to one another, regardless of time or place.

Each area that the FSA photographers covered was unique. The Dust Bowl, Pie Town, and Hispanic villages bear no outward resemblance to one another, yet the underlying truth is the same: here are honest people of the soil who worked hard and sometimes lost, but they always found a way to go on. As Ma Joad in John Steinbeck's *The Grapes of Wrath* says, "We are the people and they can't kill us." This is the heart of the FSA photographs made in New Mexico. To paraphrase William Faulkner, the people of New Mexico not only prevailed, they endured.

During the three years that I worked on this project I discovered some things about Roy Stryker that I had not realized before. We worked together for more than ten years, from 1964 to shortly before his death in 1975. When I began, I was in my early twenties. To me, Stryker was a father figure, a mentor, a famous man who had been given most of the credit for the FSA's success. I adored him and accepted at face value most of what he said. In working on this book, however, I realized that Stryker was not a saint. He was often unreasonable. He could be patronizing when addressing the plight of minorities. He altered the FSA material to suit his own ideas of what the file should be. For example, he arbitrarily punched holes in more than 100,000 negatives, not because they were technically flawed, but because he did not agree with their content.

I wondered, when rereading his letters and shooting scripts, if he were writing for posterity or for the benefit of the photographers in the field. The letters especially have a conspicuous pedagogical tone, as though Stryker were deliberately trying to ensure his place in history.

I concluded that Stryker probably needed the photographers more than they needed him. He was not a creative man, but he had a talent for organization and for making the bureaucracy work for him. He also had the ability to select the right people for the job. Walker Evans, Dorothea Lange, Russell Lee, Carl Mydans, Ben Shahn, and John Collier were already established artists when Stryker hired them. Stryker gave impetus to the project, battled continually for funds, and planted ideas in the minds of his photographers. But it was they, not he, who remained in the heartland of America month after month, year after year, making the priceless record that exists today.

As John Collier once said, "We were given tremendous leeway, but it was up to us to discover the situation and make the most of it." Russell Lee added, "Roy was a father figure. We called him when we needed money, or when we wanted to go off and do something not on the official agenda."

This book changed my perspective on New

Opposite: A homestead on a windswept prairie near Pie Town, 1986. Nancy Wood.

Mexico, too. While my work with Lee and Collier gave me the framework for this book, my field research provided authenticity. Days and weeks spent in the Dust Bowl, Pie Town, and Hispanic villages gave me a historical overview impossible to gain otherwise. I witnessed first-hand the people and the places photographed by Rothstein, Lange, Collier, and Lee. I imagined myself back in 1935 riding with Dorothea Lange in her Chevrolet coupe, seeing the terrible uprooting of a large group of rural people; I wondered what she felt when she saw the human devastation in the Dust Bowl or the slim hopes of a place like Bosque Farms. In Pie Town, I found the remains of Bill Stagg's log cabin where Russell Lee had such a good time making his pictures of a square dance. I stood in the same spot where he photographed Harmon Craig's mercantile the day the stage came through; I tried to find where Faro Caudill's dugout had been and where Faro's father had witched for water. In Peñasco, I searched for the Catholic church where Father Cassidy had said mass, but was told it had burned down years ago. I retraced John Collier's route through Las Trampas, even climbing down the side of a steep hill by Juan Lopez's house to see how Collier had managed to photograph the Lopez children chopping ice and hauling water in the dead of winter. Everywhere I went, the people immortalized by the FSA came unforgettably to life. They shared their memories, creating a bridge between me and that not-so-distant time that already is part of history.

As a result of these field experiences, my own photography began to take on a new dimension. My eye grew sharper, my feelings toward the rural people of New Mexico deeper and richer. They presented me with an opportunity to record—nearly fifty years later—circumstances not unlike those experienced by Collier and Lee. Pie Town attracted me most of all, and I went there several times simply to photograph the people and the places that form the backbone of this book. The death of Russell Lee created in me a sense of urgency about my work with these people, as well as with the Taos Pueblo Indians.

T. S. Eliot said, "Time present and time past/ Are both perhaps present in time future,/ And time future contained in time past." Nowhere is this more evident, I think, than in the rich cultural heritage of New Mexico. Here time past and time future seem arrested in time present, frozen like a paperweight scene which, when turned upside down, rains snow over everything.

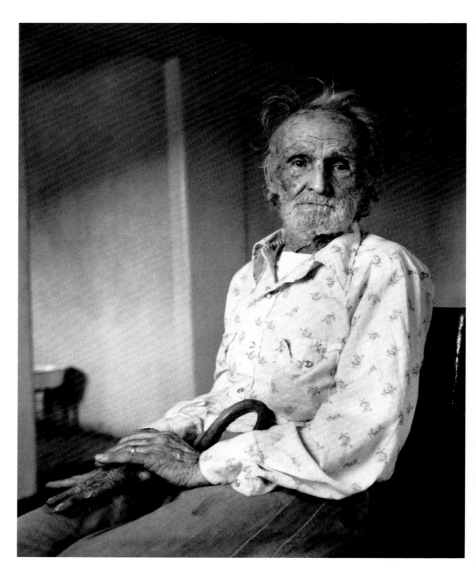

But the moment is changing. By the end of the century, the Dust Bowl town of Mills most likely will be deserted; Pie Town could well be abandoned; Las Trampas may have an entirely different character once the older generation dies off and young people move away. The FSA record is a testimonial to human courage, dignity, and strength. The judgment of the present on these photographs may indicate the values upon which our future is based. "We are all one people," Roy Stryker said to me in 1972. "I wanted to find out our connections—and our differences—that's all."

In New Mexico at least, Stryker's dream has succeeded.

Above: Edd Jones, who made Pie Town's pies during the 1930s and '40s, 1986. Nancy Wood.

NOTES ON SOURCES

Many books and articles have contributed to my knowledge of the New Deal and depression in New Mexico and the rest of the country. The works listed here represent the major sources of ideas and information obtained from other people. The book's text is a blend of this knowledge and my own, integrated with formal interviews and informal conversations I have had with people over the past twenty-five years.

Several books set the geographic and geologic stage for America's historical events from prehistoric to current times. D. W. Meinig's *Southwest* is a concise, detailed geographical history dealing with social, political, and economic changes resulting from demographic shifts in the Southwest. Focusing on a different topological area, Alexander B. Adams, in *Sunlight and Storm,* traces the background history, geology, and ecology of the Plains.

Books which focus on New Mexico include T. M. Pearce's *New Mexico Place Names,* a compendium of brief but informative facts such as location, etiology of name, and quirky stories associated with the defined town, city, land grant, or mountain range. *New Mexico: A New Guide to the Colorful State,* by Lance Chilton, Katherine Chilton, Polly E. Arango, et al., is an updated version of the guide written by WPA workers in 1940. This edition, covering the period from World War II to the present, is full of historical fact, geographical description, anecdotes, drawings, photographs, and maps, providing an excellent three-dimensional overview. The second edition of Jerry L. Williams's *New Mexico in Maps* is a cornucopia of facts about New Mexico from Paleozoic paleontology to presidential elections.

Two of many books concerning the depression and New Deal provided a general overview within which to set New Mexico's history during that time period. Donald Worster's *Dust Bowl* is a critical survey of the causes and cures of the Dust Bowl, with special emphasis on the human interest element. Paul Bonnifield's *The Dust Bowl* is a scholarly yet readable social history narrative which focuses on communities in Oklahoma, Kansas, and Colorado and on Mills, New Mexico.

A variety of books deal with various aspects of New Mexico history. Marc Simmons's *New Mexico* is a summary of significant events in the state's history and an excellent source for the reader who wants a general overview rather than great detail. A good companion volume, also by Simmons, is *Albuquerque,* a greatly detailed account of the city's history. In *The Missions of New Mexico Since 1776,* John L. Kessell traces the histories and architectural modifications of the thirty-two missions described by Fray Francisco Atanasio Dominguez in 1776. The book is rich in fact as well as lively anecdotes which breathe life into each mission.

In *Penitente Self-Government,* Thomas J. Steele and Rowena T. Rivera have written a clear, scholarly study of how and why the Penitente Brotherhood came into existence, and why it survived. In *Chimayo Valley Traditions,* Elizabeth Kay gives an anecdotal account of religious practices around the Chimayo region. Charles Aranda's *Dichos* gives insight into Hispanic culture and beliefs through the sayings of the people. In *Survival of Spanish American Villages,* Paul Kutsche gives a first-rate anthropological analysis of the decline of New Mexico's Hispanic villages in the twentieth century.

William de Buys's book, *Enchantment and Exploitation,* is the definitive work on the history, ecology, spiritual legacy, and complex land grant issues of the southern Sangre de Cristo Mountains. He also provides an excellent discourse on the history of Las Trampas. Ferenc Szasz's *The Day the Sun Rose Twice* describes events leading up to and following development of the atom bomb in Los Alamos, New Mexico. It is a riveting account and contributes to an understanding of the impact of the nuclear age on New Mexico and the rest of the nation.

I used several sources for information on the New Deal in New Mexico. William Pickens's Master's thesis, "The New Deal in New Mexico," is an excellent critique of the origin and consequences of New Deal programs in New Mexico. An even more detailed version of this thesis may be found in Pickens's "The New Deal in New Mexico," in John Braeman, Robert H. Bremner, and David Brody's book, *The New Deal*. In *Hispanic Villages of Northern New Mexico*, Marta Weigle has made a valuable contribution to New Mexico's history by reprinting the 1935 Tewa Basin Study conducted by the U.S. government, which discussed cultural and environmental factors affecting the people of northern New Mexico villages during the depression. In *It Happened in Taos*, J. T. Reid tells about the problems experienced by the people of Taos County during the depression, and what communal efforts were made to solve those problems. In *Native Americans in the Twentieth Century*, James S. Olson and Raymond Wilson write about major issues of concern and consequence to contemporary Native Americans, including the Indian New Deal.

Two articles contributed to my understanding of Pie Town: Toby Smith's "Pie Town: A Trip Back" and L. Meyer's "Pie Town: Last Homesteading Community."

Alfred N. Chandler's *Land Title Origins* is a detailed study of Spanish land grants and their uses and misuses. Clark S. Knowlton's *Land-Grant Problems Among the State's Spanish Americans* is a searing account of corruption involved in the land grant issue.

Of the profusion of books about photographers and photographs from the depression and New Deal era, F. Jack Hurley's *A Portrait of a Decade* is the most scholarly and complete book on Stryker's role in the Farm Security Administration. In *A Vision Shared*, Hank O'Neal makes a valuable analysis of the individual photographers' work in the Farm Security Administration. In *Documentary Photography* Arthur Rothstein thoroughly examines the documentary tradition.

Robert Coles and Alex Harris's *The Old Ones of New Mexico* is a powerful social commentary on elderly Hispanic residents of northern New Mexican villages, often using the people's own words. *Russell Lee's F.S.A.: Photographs of Chamisal and Peñasco*, edited by William Wroth, is a revealing account of Lee's work in northern New Mexico and includes an excellent history of the area by Charles A. Briggs.

Much of the information used in this book comes from my interviews with Roy Stryker, 1964–70; John Collier, Jr., 1985–87; and Russell Lee, 1985–86. In addition, I spoke with residents of Mills, Springer, and Bosque Farms, February–March 1987; with residents of Pie Town, 1985–86; with residents of Las Trampas, Rodarte, and Taos County, February–April 1987; and with Father Walter Cassidy, March 1987.

BIBLIOGRAPHY

Adams, Alexander B. *Sunlight and Storm: The Great American Plains.* New York: Putnam, 1977.

Agee, James, and Walker Evans. *Let Us Now Praise Famous Men.* Boston: Houghton Mifflin, 1941.

Anderson, Sherwood. *Home Town: The Face of America.* New York: Alliance, 1941.

Aranda, Charles. *Dichos: Proverbs and Sayings from the Spanish.* Santa Fe: Sunstone, 1975.

Baldwin, Sidney. *Poverty and Politics: The Rise and Decline of the Farm Security Administration.* Chapel Hill: University of North Carolina Press, 1968.

Bonnifield, Paul. *The Dust Bowl: Men, Dirt and Depression.* Albuquerque: University of New Mexico Press, 1979.

Braeman, John, Robert H. Bremner, David Brody, eds. *The New Deal: The State and Local Levels.* 2 vols. Columbus: Ohio State University Press, 1975.

Brown, Lorin W., with Charles L. Briggs and Marta Weigle. *Hispano Folklife of New Mexico: The Lorin W. Brown Federal Writers' Project Manuscripts.* Albuquerque: University of New Mexico Press, 1978.

Caldwell, Erskine, and Margaret Bourke-White. *You Have Seen Their Faces.* New York: Modern Age Books, 1937.

Chamberlain, Samuel, ed. *Fair Is Our Land.* Chicago: Peoples Book Club, 1942.

Chandler, Alfred N. *Land Title Origins: A Tale of Force and Fraud.* New York: Robert Schalkenbach Foundation, 1945.

Chilton, Lance, Katherine Chilton, Polly E. Arango, James Dudley, Nancy Neary, Patricia Stelzner. *New Mexico: A New Guide to the Colorful State.* Albuquerque: University of New Mexico Press, 1984.

Coles, Robert, and Alex Harris. *The Old Ones of New Mexico.* Albuquerque: University of New Mexico Press, 1973.

Collier, John. *From Every Zenith: A Memoir.* Denver: Sage Books, 1963.

————. *Indians of the Americas: The Long Hope.* New York: Mentor, 1947.

Collier, John, Jr. *Visual Anthropology: Photography as a Research Method.* New York: Holt, Rinehart and Winston, 1967.

Conkin, Paul. *Tomorrow a New World: The New Deal Community Program.* Ithaca, N.Y.: Cornell University Press, 1959.

Conrad, David E. *The Forgotten Farmers: The Story of Sharecroppers in the New Deal.* Urbana: University of Illinois Press, 1965.

Daniel, Pete, ed. *America in the Depression Years: Master Guide.* Laurel, Md.: Instructional Resources, 1979.

De Buys, William. *Enchantment and Exploitation: The Life and Hard Times of a New Mexico Mountain Range.* Albuquerque: University of New Mexico Press, 1985.

Dixon, Penelope. *Photographers of the Farm Security Administration: An Annotated Bibliography 1930–1980.* New York: Garland, 1983.

Donnelly, Thomas C. *Government of New Mexico.* Albuquerque: University of New Mexico Press, 1947.

Dozier, Edward P. *The Pueblo Indians of North America.* New York: Holt, Rinehart and Winston, 1970.

Evans, Walker. *American Photographs.* New York: Museum of Modern Art, 1938.

Ferris, Bill. *Images of the South: Visits with Eudora Welty and Walker Evans.* Memphis: Center for Southern Folklore, 1977.

First Annual Report of the Resettlement Administration. Washington, D.C.: U.S. Government Documents, 1936.

Gabriel, Bertram. "W.P.A. Murals—Fine Art from Hard Times." *New Mexico Magazine* (November 1982): 16–22.

Garver, Thomas H., ed. *Just Before the War: Urban America Seen by Photographers of the Farm Security Administration.* Los Angeles: Rapid Lithograph, 1968.

Hewett, Edgar L., and Bertha P. Dutton. *The Pueblo Indian World.* Santa Fe: School of American Research, 1945.

Holmes, Jack E. *Politics of New Mexico.* Albuquerque: University of New Mexico Press, 1967.

Horgan, Paul. *The Heroic Triad: Backgrounds of Our Three Southwestern Cultures.* New York: Holt, Rinehart and Winston, 1970.

Howard, Donald S. *The W.P.A. and Federal Relief Policy.* New York: Russell Sage Foundation, 1943.

Hurley, F. Jack. *Portrait of a Decade: Roy Stryker and the Development of Documentary Photography in the Thirties.* Baton Rouge: Louisiana State University Press, 1972.

————. *Russell Lee, Photographer.* Dobbs Ferry, N.Y.: Morgan & Morgan, 1978.

Kay, Elizabeth. *Chimayo Valley Traditions.* Santa Fe: Ancient City, 1987.

Kelly, Lawrence C. *The Assault on Assimilation: John Collier and the Origins of Indian Policy Reform.* Albuquerque: University of New Mexico Press, 1983.

Kessell, John L. *The Missions of New Mexico Since 1776.* Albuquerque: University of New Mexico Press, 1980.

Knowlton, Clark S. "Land-Grant Problems Among the State's Spanish-Americans." *New Mexico Business* 20 (June 1967): 1–13.

Kutsche, Paul. *Survival of Spanish-American Villages.* Colorado Springs: Research Committee, Colorado College, 1979.

Lange, Dorothea. *Dorothea Lange.* Millerton, N.Y.: Aperture, 1981.

————. *Dorothea Lange Looks at the American Country Woman.* Ft. Worth: Amon Carter Museum, 1967.

————, and Paul Schuster Taylor. *An American Exodus: A Recession of Human Erosion.* New York: Reynal & Hitchkok, 1939.

Leuchtenburg, William E. *Franklin D. Roosevelt and the New Deal.* New York: Harper & Row, 1963.

Lowitt, Richard. *The New Deal and the West.* Bloomington: Indiana University Press, 1984.

Lynd, Robert S., and Helen M. Lynd. *Middletown: A Study in American Culture.* New York: Harcourt, Brace and Co., 1929.

MacLeish, Archibald. *Land of the Free.* New York: Harcourt, Brace and Co., 1938.

McCamy, James L. *Government Publicity—Its Practice in Federal Administration.* Chicago: University of Chicago Press, 1939.

McDonald, William F. *Federal Relief Administration and the Arts.* Columbus: Ohio State University Press, 1969.

McElvaine, Robert S. *The Great Depression: America, 1929–1941.* New York: Times Books, 1984.

McKinzie, Richard D. *The New Deal for Artists.* Princeton: Princeton University Press, 1973.

McNitt, Frank. *Navajo Wars.* Albuquerque: University of New Mexico Press, 1972.

Meinig, D. W. *Southwest: Three Peoples in Geographical Change 1600–1970.* New York: Oxford University Press, 1971.

Meyer, L. "Pie Town: Last Homesteading Community." *American Heritage* 31 (February/March 1980): 74–81.

Moley, Raymond. *After Seven Years.* New York: Harper and Bros., 1939.

Nash, Gerald D. *Great Depression and the New Deal.* New York: St. Martin's, 1979.

Newhall, Beaumont. *The History of Photography.* New York: Museum of Modern Art, 1970.

New Mexico: A Guide to the Colorful State. Compiled by workers of the Writers' Program of the Work Projects Administration, Coronado Cuarto Centennial Commission. New York: American Guide Series, Hastings House, 1940.

Nixon, Herman Clarence. *Forty Acres and Steel Mules.* Chapel Hill: University of North Carolina Press, 1938.

O'Connor, Francis V. *Federal Support for the Visual Arts: The New Deal and Now.* Greenwich, Conn.: New York Graphic Society, 1969.

————. *Ohio, A Photographic Portrait, 1935–1941: Farm Security Administration Photographs.* Akron, Ohio: Akron Art Institute; distributed by Kent State University Press, 1980.

Olson, James S., and Raymond Wilson. *Native Americans in the Twentieth Century.* Urbana: University of Illinois Press, 1984.

O'Neal, Hank. *A Vision Shared: A Classic Portrait of America and Its People, 1935–1943.* New York: St. Martin's Press, 1976.

Parman, Donald. *The Navajos and the New Deal.* New Haven: Yale University Press, 1979.

Patterson, James T. *The New Deal and the States.* Westport, Conn.: Greenwood Press, 1969.

Pearce, T. M. *New Mexico Place Names: A Geographical Dictionary.* Albuquerque: University of New Mexico Press, 1965.

Pickens, William Hickman. "The New Deal in New Mexico: Changes in State Government and Politics 1926–1938." M.A. thesis. University of New Mexico, 1971.

Raper, Arthur F. *Preface to Peasantry: A Tale of Two Black Belt Counties.* Chapel Hill: University of North Carolina Press, 1936.

————, with Farm Security Administration; photographs by Jack Delano. *Tenants of the Almighty.* New York: Arno Press, 1971.

Reid, J. T. *It Happened in Taos.* Albuquerque: University of New Mexico Press, 1946.

Riis, Jacob. *How the Other Half Lives.* New York: Scribner, 1890.

————. *The Making of an American.* New York: Macmillan Co., 1901.

Rodman, Selden. *Portrait of the Artist as an American. Ben Shahn: A Biography with Pictures.* New York: Harper, 1949.

Rothstein, Arthur. *The Depression Years.* New York: Dover Publications, 1978.

————. *Documentary Photography.* Stoneham, Mass.: Focal Press, 1986.

Saunders, Lyle. *A Guide to Materials Bearing on Cultural Relations in New Mexico.* Albuquerque: University of New Mexico Press, 1944.

Schlesinger, Arthur M., Jr. *The Age of Roosevelt: The Crisis of the Old Order, 1919–1933.* Boston: Houghton Mifflin, 1957.

Scholes, France V. *Troublous Times in New Mexico, 1659–1670.* Albuquerque: University of New Mexico Press, 1942.

Shahn, Ben. *Ben Shahn, Photographer: An Album from the Thirties.* New York: Da Capo Press, 1973.

Simmons, Marc. *Albuquerque: A Narrative History.* Albuquerque: University of New Mexico Press, 1982.

————. *New Mexico: A Bicentennial History.* New York: W. W. Norton, 1977.

Smith, Toby. "Pie Town: A Trip Back." *Impact Magazine, Albuquerque Journal,* January 18, 1983.

Sonnichsen, C. L. *The Mescalero Apaches.* Norman: University of Oklahoma Press, 1958.

Steele, Thomas J., and Rowena A. Rivera. *Penitente Self-Government: Brotherhoods and Councils 1797–1947.* Santa Fe: Ancient City, 1985.

Steichen, Edward, ed. *The Bitter Years, 1935–1941: Rural America as Seen by the Photographers of the Farm Security Administration.* New York: Museum of Modern Art, 1962.

Stryker, Roy E., and Nancy Wood. *In This Proud Land.* Boston: New York Graphic Society, 1974.

Szasz, Ferenc. *The Day the Sun Rose Twice.* Albuquerque: University of New Mexico Press, 1984.

Thomas, Alfred B. *Forgotten Frontiers.* Norman: University of Oklahoma Press, 1932.

Tugwell, Rexford G. *The Brains Trust*. New York: Viking Press, 1968.

————, Thomas Munro, and Roy E. Stryker. *American Economic Life*. New York: Harcourt, Brace, 1925.

U.S. Library of Congress, Prints and Photographs Division. *Walker Evans: Photographs for the Farm Security Administration, 1935–1938*. New York: Da Capo Press, 1973.

Vance, Rupert B. *How the Other Half Is Housed: A Pictorial Record of Sub-Minimum Farm Housing in the South*. Chapel Hill: University of North Carolina Press, 1936.

Weigle, Marta, with Mary Powell. "From Alice Corbin's 'Lines Mumbled in Sleep' to 'Eufemia's Sopapillas': Women and the Federal Writers' Project in New Mexico." *New America: A Journal of American and Southwestern Culture* 4 (1982): 54–76.

————, ed. *Hispanic Villages of Northern New Mexico: A Reprint of Volume II of the 1935 Tewa Basin Study, with Supplementary Materials*. Santa Fe: Lightning Tree, 1975.

Whitman, William, III. *The Pueblo Indians of San Ildefonso: A Changing Culture*. New York: Columbia University, 1947.

Williams, Jerry L., ed. *New Mexico in Maps*. 2nd ed. Albuquerque: University of New Mexico Press, 1986.

Worster, Donald. *Dust Bowl: The Southern Plains in the 1930s*. New York: Oxford University Press, 1979.

Wroth, William, ed. *Russell Lee's F.S.A. Photographs of Chamisal and Peñasco*. Santa Fe: Ancient City, 1985.

The Years of Bitterness and Pride: Farm Security Administration Photographs, 1935–1943. New York: McGraw-Hill, 1975.

Zielinski, John. *Unknown Iowa: Farm Security Photos, 1936–1941*. Kalona, Iowa: Photo-Art Gallery Publications, 1977.